THE SNAKE HAS ALL THE LINES

BY JEAN KERR

THE SNAKE HAS ALL THE LINES
PLEASE DON'T EAT THE DAISIES

Co-author of:

GOLDILOCKS
KING OF HEARTS

THE SNAKE

BY JEAN KERR

HAS ALL THE LINES

WITH DRAWINGS BY WHITNEY DARROW, JR.

DOUBLEDAY & COMPANY, INC., GARDEN CITY, NEW YORK 1960

For TOM and KITTY—with love

NOTES AND ACKNOWLEDGMENTS

I wish to thank Miss Helen L. Carson (of Elizabeth, New Jersey), who was kind enough to read this book in manuscript and make a number of suggestions. Nevertheless, I felt it ought to be published. Surely we *need* books of substance. As for Miss Carson's attitude toward my materials ("Just because these things *exist,* do we have to talk about them?"), I can only say that I consider this dangerous escapism and muddy thinking. I doubt very much if that girl will ever broaden her horizons.

I have written an inspirational book for one reason only. I wanted to help. These are troubled times. Historywise, we are at the crossroads. I sense a desperate need for the kind of constructive thinking that sweeps away cobwebs. This book, then, is intended to fill a long-felt need, particularly among thoughtful people who are prone to introspection and find themselves wondering from time to time why they bother to get out of bed in the morning.

It may be suggested that I have chewed up more than I ever bit off. (Try to help some people and all you get is criticism.) But if I have brought a word of encouragement to even one hundred thousand people I shall be satisfied.

Of course, there are a number of individuals in this country who are so superbly adjusted that they do not require assistance. And I am not thinking of Leonard Bernstein, I am thinking of a friend of mine who lives in Washington, D.C.

Ginny was always a charming, vivacious girl, but when I last saw her, ten years ago, she was definitely on the frumpy side. Imagine my surprise when I met her at the Shoreham last week looking absolutely dazzling in a red taffeta ball gown. I was startled right out of my manners and blurted, "Ginny, you look marvelous—what happened?" She didn't seem disconcerted by my bluntness. She smiled sweetly and said, in the cheeriest tones imaginable, "Why, honey, two things happened to me. I lost weight, and I got rich." There, that's what I call inspiring. I mean, what else *is* there?

On the other hand, what do most of us find at the end of the rainbow? Another rainbow. Disillusionment stalks us all. Even children discover at a tender age that we have no permanent kingdom, and all is tinsel.

For example, our Christopher came home from school one day to announce, in a rather apathetic manner, that the first grade was putting on a play about Adam and Eve and he had been cast as Adam. I was mystified by his lack of enthusiasm and I said, "You're playing Adam? Why, that's wonderful, that's the *lead!*" "Yeah," he replied gloomily, "but the *snake* has all the lines."

Now isn't that the case all over? You work, you slave. Honors seem just within reach. And what do find? The snake has all the lines.

CONTENTS

13

THE SNAKE HAS ALL THE LINES

I WAS A SAND CRAB

I make mistakes; I'll be the second to admit it. For instance, I will buy anything—*anything*—that has been reduced to one third of its original price. I now own, among other things, a wonderful emergency repair kit for patching up plastic swimming pools, which was an absolute steal at ninety-eight cents and which will doubtless prove invaluable when and if we get a plastic swimming pool. And just last week I bought a brown shantung dress at Saks Fifth Avenue for twenty-eight dollars (a fraction of its former price) which, on closer inspection, seems to give me the distinction and the interesting contours of a large bran muffin. Of course the dress is not a total loss, because for the first time in my life I have something that's fit to wear shopping in Saks Fifth Avenue.

But there's one mistake I've never made. I have never taken our children on an extended vacation. I understand that other people do it all the time. They pack up the whole brood (and Nutsy the dog) and go camping in the Canadian Rockies, or, with Daddy at the helm, they sail around Cape Horn on an old sand barge. Not only that, but they have enough energy left over to write a book about it. It all sounds so jolly. I find myself speechless with admiration as I read: "Oh, what a breakfast that was! Skipper and Dad came home with their catch, a brace of gleaming sunfish, and noted with approval that the four-year-old twins had already built a roaring fire in the grate. Susie made several loaves of her special Indian-meal bread, and Little Joe, our toddler, crept around the roughhewn table, spreading the large ferns that were to serve as table mats." Now there's an integrated little group—and talk about teamwork! Of course, that mother doesn't seem to have lifted a finger. But then, she wrote the book, and that takes it out of you.

Up to now the farthest we've ever taken all five children is to the mailbox on the corner. We do, however, take them to the beach—which is closer than the mailbox, being directly across the road. And I have discovered that those long, hot afternoons on the sand can be fun for young and old, provided you keep your wits about you.

The first time I took our boys to the beach I was so naïve that I actually brought along a copy of Sheed's *Theology and Sanity*. It was my plan to loll in the deck chair and improve my mind while the happy children gamboled and frolicked on the sand. That was my plan. *Their* plan was to show me two dead crabs, five clam shells, one rusty pail they found under two rocks, the two rocks, two hundred and seventy-two Good Humor sticks, one small boy who had taken off his bathing suit, one enormous hole they dug (and wasn't it lucky the life guard fell in it, and not the old gentleman in braces), fourteen cigarette butts, and a tear in Gilbert's new bathing trunks.

I don't mean that it's impossible to read, but you do have to select the reading material with some care. *Theology and Sanity* is out, and so is any book in which the author writes an introduction acknowledging his indebtedness to more than thirty-eight sources. The ideal thing would be a mail-order catalogue, or, if you insist on narrative, there is a wonderful little Golden Book about a boy named Timmy who wanted to be a choo-choo.

Speaking about dead crabs, I have found it advisable when presented with any species of marine life, no matter how advanced in decay, to assume that it is still alive. In this way you can appeal to the children's nobler nature. I have stood, as close as my nose would allow, over the ghastly carcass of some unlovely denizen of the deep (now clearly past the reach of all wonder drugs) and muttered sagely, "The thing is, darling, he seems dead because he's scared." [*He's* scared?] "He's just lonesome, so why don't

you put him back in the water and let him swim with his
brothers and sisters?" It's better this way, really. Otherwise
they will take him home to bury him, which would be all
right if they buried him. But they don't bury him—they
leave him in the garage or in a wastebasket in the bathroom. I know one little boy—in fact, he's related to me—
who once put an enormous dead horseshoe crab in the Ben-
dix. As a matter of fact, it couldn't have been that enormous
or I'd have noticed it before I put in all those sheets.

It's a simple enough matter to sit back and admire the
constant stream of salvage that the little ones dump in your
lap. You need only the vivacity of Arlene Francis, the un-
failing cheer of Ralph Edwards, and the natural instinct
for hyperbole of an ad man working on a new toothpaste
account. You must be careful, though, not to shoot your
bolt on sea shells. Save a little enthusiasm for when you
have to watch them "swim." You don't want to break down
completely, like one harassed father I heard bellowing at
his four-year-old, "I don't call that swimming, Ralphie—
I call that *walking!*"

For the record, Ralphie was certainly walking, but he
had a magnificent overhand splash, and around here we
give points for that. If you are given a choice, it is much
less taxing to watch them swim under water than over
water, because you don't have to shout encouragements
while they are actually submerged. In fact you can more
or less think your own thoughts until they reappear. The
demonstrations, however, had better take place in very
shallow water—otherwise, if they're one second late in re-

appearing, your own thoughts may give you a heart attack.

We come now to the subject of discipline at the beach. Personally, I marvel at how calm other mothers stay (I'm told it has something to do with the presence of B_1 vitamins in the diet). Recently I heard one tranquil lady gently admonishing her son, "Brucie, I don't think you should pour water on that lady until she changes into her bathing suit." And when Brucie continued to pour, his mother played what was clearly her trump card and said firmly, "Very well—you go right on doing that and you'll see!" This worried me. That large, fully clothed, damp lady was carrying a purse, and she might, just possibly, have had a gun.

When I see my boys dropping wet seaweed on somebody's sound-asleep face or spilling sand into an open jar of cold cream, I simply shout, "Little boy! Stop that immediately or I will ask your father to spank you!" This stops him without exactly revealing my true identity as the parent of the delinquent.

It's nice when the whole family goes to the beach together and you can occasionally turn the kids over to their alternate sponsor, Daddy. Otherwise you may go the whole summer burned only on one side. There is just one difficulty: fathers are even more trouble at the shore than small children. For one thing, fathers are nervous. There are fathers who can detect menacing possibilities in the spectacle of a four-month-old infant lying flat in the exact middle of a perfectly clean, perfectly bare 9 x 12 rug.

Take such a man to the beach and you have a really

classic bundle of nerves, sensitive as a piece of gold leaf, alert to every danger, suspicious of the hostile elements of sea and air, ready always to defend the nest. He demonstrates his vigilance by asking a series of hoarse, rhetorical questions: "Should Col be out that far? Do you let John climb up on those rocks, come *down* off there, you idiot! Don't you think Gilbert should go home, he's blue. Doesn't that kid have a bathing suit that fits him? Good Lord, did we pay forty bucks to teach him to swim like *that?*"

Another thing. If you want stability in a marriage, it is obviously wiser to work out any policy involving the children in advance. For instance, I think you should know before you leave the house just how many times you are prepared to replace ice-cream cones that topple off into the sand. Twice, three times—it doesn't matter, so long as both parents are agreed. If you haven't taken this precaution there are apt to be painful little scenes, with Daddy saying,

"Sooner or later that kid has got to learn how to hold onto it," and Mommy muttering, "Poor little lamb—they just don't push them *down* far enough."

I don't know whether children actually do make more loud, embarrassing statements at the beach than in other public places or whether it merely seems that way because the acoustics are better. Once, in a crowded subway where he couldn't be heard anyway, our four-year-old pointed to a highly painted lady who was clearly no lady and said, rather winningly I thought, "Oh, Mommy, see her pink cheeks—she must eat a lot of carrots!" But at the beach all chivalry vanishes. The same child will stare at the kindly gentleman who has just smiled at him and ask in clarion tones, "Why has he got black hair on his head and white hair on his chest?" Which is one reason why I wear very dark glasses and very large sun hats even on overcast days.

Sometimes I can sense an unfortunate remark in the

making (for instance, when the woman walking toward us looks pretty peculiar to me too) and I can forestall it by the simple device of saying, "Here, I bet you can't get this whole banana into your mouth at once." But the day comes when, in spite of all your precautions, one of them will spot the oldest and most venerable member of the community and sing out at concert pitch, "Mommy, is that man a lady?"

What you do then is just pack up everything and go home. And that's no hardship, really. After all, what does a day at the beach do for you? It just brings out all your freckles and ruins a perfectly good three-dollar hair set.

LETTERS OF PROTEST I NEVER SENT

It seems to me that I used to sleep better before we had all these conveniences. Lately I find that just as I am sinking into that first sweet slumber of the night I suddenly remember I forgot to take a leg of lamb out of the freezer. At this point I have two clear alternatives. I can pad down to the garage and get the lamb, or I can lie there and figure out what else we could have for dinner tomorrow night (hamburger or what five-year-old Gilbert calls "creamed chipped beast").

Either way I'm now fully awake, bright-eyed, alert. Indeed there seems to be a penetrating sharpness to my mind, a quickness that I never notice in the daytime. At this moment I feel that I could be profitably reading Toynbee's *A Study of History* or the directions on the Waring Blendor.

The problem is, of course, to channel this alarming mental energy before I lapse back into that old, and disastrous, habit of reviewing the low points of my life (the night I swallowed an inlay in the Oak Room at the Plaza, the day I dropped—and smashed—a large bottle of mineral oil in the elevator of the Time-Life Building, the Sunday that Honey, our cocker spaniel, ate my mother-in-law's wrist watch).

It was only recently that I discovered that one could put this otherwise lost time to work and make it pay off in terms of mental health, which, I am sure we are all agreed, becomes more elusive all the time. Now I just make a list of all the tiny irritations that have been nibbling away at my subconscious, and I compose dignified letters of protest. (Major irritations, like plumbers who come and make extensive repairs on the wrong bathtub and dry cleaners who press boys' jackets without removing the chocolate kisses from the pockets, I omit on the theory that these really require a stern phone call.) I find that after I have written one of these letters mentally I forget the whole matter, and the next day my mind is clear to grapple with real problems, like where on earth I put all those Halloween costumes last November.

And, actually, these nocturnal doodlings hurt nobody. I never do type them up in the morning because I'm too sluggish and, on the various occasions when I suggested that I might really mail one of them, my husband has always stopped me by asking a simple question: "Are you out of your mind?"

I am putting down a few sample letters here in case there is another insomniac somewhere who would like to be as disagreeable as possible (without repercussions) but hasn't quite got the hang of it:

The Ever-Krisp Curtain Co.,
Dear Sirs:

In what mad burst of whimsy did you adopt the slogan "These curtains laugh at soap and water"? Now, I begrudge no man his flights of fancy. We are all poets at heart. And when I purchased my Ever-Krisp curtains I did not really expect them to burst into wild guffaws or even ladylike giggles the first time I put them in the sink. (As a matter of fact, with five small boys and one loud Siamese cat, I don't want to hear one word from those curtains.) But, in my incurable naïveté, I did take your claim to imply that these curtains actually survived contact with soap and water. I don't mean I expect them to remain everkrisp. I'm quite accustomed to ever-limp curtains. I did, however, expect them to remain ever-red with ever-white ruffles. As it happens, they are now a sort of off-pink strawberry ripple, which of course doesn't go with my kitchen at all.

Ever-Disgusted

Acme Novelty Co.,
Dear Sirs:

I am writing to you about your water guns. They
leak. And not out of the muzzle, which would be logi-
cal, but out of the top because the little stopper
doesn't fit. And if you put the gun under your pillow
(naturally, I don't put it under my pillow) the water
seeps out and wets the whole mattress.

I really can't imagine why you discontinued the
plastic model you featured last year. This was an admirable, indeed an ideal, water gun. It worked perfectly for fifteen minutes and then broke into two
equal halves. It was worth twenty-five cents. I wish
I could say the same for this year's model.

Distressed Consumer

The Pilgrim Laundry,
Dear Sirs:

For years I've rather admired the crisp little mes-
sages that appear on that paper strip that is wrapped
around the shirts when they come back from your
laundry. The sentiments expressed may not have been
very original or very imaginative (Merry Christmas,
Have a safe Fourth of July) but one felt there was a
nice spirit there, and if the tone was sometimes a
shade dogmatic it was never carping.

Well, gentlemen, you must try to imagine my shock
when, last week, I discovered the new message which

29

read "*Have you kissed your wife this morning?*" I don't know what you call this, but I call it prying. Furthermore, my husband never sees these wrappers because I tear them off before I pile the shirts in the drawer. And since I don't have a wife, I feel like an impostor and a perfect idiot.

Because I have a sincere interest in consumer research, and kisses, I decided to show one of these strips to my husband and test his reaction. What he said was (and these are exact quotes), "*You tell that laundry that if I had a wife who ironed my shirts I'd kiss her.*"

Now, Pilgrims, think! Surely you never meant to stir up that little kettle of fish. Not only does it lead to apartness, or whatever is the opposite of togetherness, but one sees how easily it could boomerang on the whole laundry business. You were just trying to help, I know that. But let me suggest that you concentrate on those shirts. Would you sew the buttons back on and try not to press the wrinkles into the collars, please?

Thanks

To a Columnist,
Dear Sir:

In a recent column you ran the item, "*What titled English actor is serious about a current aquatic star (initials L.D.) now hitting the bottle?*" Well, this was

a real puzzler. I was able to figure out the English actor part easily enough by getting hold of a copy of Burke's Peerage. But that current aquatic star (initials L.D.) has me stumped. I admit I just don't keep up on things (it was July Fourth before I discovered that June was National Dairy Month) but even so, I feel I would have noticed the emergence of a new swimmer named Lorna Doone (Lola Duprez? Lana Durner?). I used to know a girl in Wilkes-Barre named Lorraine Dickson who was a marvelous swimmer, but she uses her married name now, which is Ruffo. Anyway, she wouldn't be hitting the bottle because she has only one kidney and she doesn't drink at all. I will be anxiously watching your column for further details.

Baffled Reader (initials J.K.)

31

Bergdorf Goodman,
Dear Sirs:

In Sunday's paper you had an advertisement for "a casual little go-everywhere frock @ $125." Now what I want to know is, just exactly how casual is this dress? I mean, it isn't too casual, is it? Would it really give one a feeling of social security and a sense of "belonging" in the A&P? If you wore it to Parents' Night and had to talk to the principal, would it perhaps seem just a trifle slapdash?

Bergdorf's, oh Bergdorf's, can you hear me? You must come down off that mountaintop. I'm afraid you've been overprotected. People you trusted have been keeping things from you. Promise you won't get mad if I tell you something: you're on the wrong track. I know women who spend that kind of money on clothes. (Well, I don't exactly know them, I overhear them talking during the intermissions at First Nights.) But I feel myself to be on solid ground when I say that, @ $125, they're not looking for a frock, they're looking for a dress and one that would make Lanvin-Castillo think twice.

Are we still friends?

Little Cinema Movie Theater,
Dear Sirs:

I called your theater yesterday afternoon and I said to the woman who answered the phone, "Young lady—" (*from her voice I judged her to be at least sixty-five but I wanted to get on her good side*) *"young lady," I said, "will you please tell me at what time this evening you are showing* La Strada. *Also, please tell me at what time you are showing* Jailhouse Rock *with Elvis Presley." I was very calm. I didn't prejudice the case. Nor did I reveal by any hint of hysteria which picture I was trying to avoid. Anyway she told me that* La Strada *began at 8:10 and* Jailhouse Rock *began at 10:16. Not satisfied with this (I am unnaturally cautious ever since I saw, as a result of circumstances beyond my control, a picture called* Ten Thousand Bedrooms), *I called back in five minutes and, in an assumed southern accent (which I do rather well, having once played an end man in a minstrel show), I asked the same question and got the same answer. It was, then, with complete confidence that my husband and I arrived at the theater at 8:10 to discover the opening credits of* Jailhouse Rock *rolling onto the screen. Now this may seem a very trifling mistake to you, but I assure you that my husband is a very nervous man (of course, he wasn't this nervous before* Jailhouse Rock) *and his condition has worsened noticeably. Little things, like the children banging the basketball against the plate-glass doors, that he used to be able to pass off with a joke and a smile now reduce him to screaming and shouting. This you must put on your conscience, Little Cinema. You may ask why we didn't leave and come back for* La

Strada. *Well, for one thing we had already parked the car, and my husband didn't feel that at his age he could walk up and down in front of the theater with that big bag of popcorn—and he wouldn't throw it away.*

Aggrieved Moviegoer

Dear Sister Saint Joseph:

Colin tells me that he is playing the part of the Steering Wheel in the Safety play. He feels, as do I, that he could bring a lot more to the part of the Stop Sign. I know Stop Sign is a speaking part, and while I realize that Colin is not ready for "leads," still he did memorize all three stanzas of "America, the Beautiful," and I myself would have absolute confidence in his ability to handle the line "I am the Stop Sign, I am here to help you," which I understand consti-

tutes the whole part. Also, Colin is very tall for seven and I'm sure we're agreed that height is very important for this role. Finally, let me mention (although I do not expect it to influence your decision in any way) that I just happen to have a Stop Sign costume which I made for his brother three years ago.

Cordially,
Colin's Mother

Dear Doctor Murphy:

Those new sleeping pills that you said would "fell an ox" don't work either. Now what will I do?

Desperately,
Jean

GO, JOSEPHINE,
IN YOUR FLYING MACHINE

I feel about airplanes the way I feel about diets. It seems to me that they are wonderful things for other people to go on. When a friend of mine decides to fly to Milwaukee, I drive her out to La Guardia with marvelous calm and equanimity. I am positively lighthearted in the knowledge that she will receive loving, tender care and arrive with every curl intact. Lightning may be cracking around us, but I am calm.

"Nonsense, Josephine," I say, clasping her perspiring

palm, "it's the *only* way to go." Whereupon I deliver a brisk lecture on the statistics of safety in air travel. Indeed, if my figures are correct the only possible way you could be injured in an airplane is by inadvertently strangling yourself with the seat belt.

If my departing friend continues to be pessimistic about the lowering sky and the leaden clouds, I get just a wee bit impatient. "Honestly," I say, supported by the facts and good common sense, "you *are* a fuddy-duddy. This is the twentieth century, for heaven's sake. You'll get there right on time." And I'm right, of course. She always gets there, frequently before I get back home from the airport, what with the tie-up of traffic on the Whitestone Bridge.

When I fly, it's a different story altogether. In the first place, I am a rational human being and I'm not the least bit interested in statistics. I happen to know that planes do crash. *You* see those pictures in the paper—the smoking ruins, the dazed survivors, the pilot (when he is able to answer questions at St. Vincent's Hospital) reporting, "All I know is that two of the engines conked out." And please don't tell me a lot of irrelevant stories about train wrecks and auto collisions. The fact remains that I have been driving in cars and riding on trains all my life and nothing has ever happened to me. And you can't say as much for planes. All kinds of things have happened to me on planes.

So the day before a flight I always revise my will and write short notes of maternal guidance to each of my children. (These will be found in the top bureau drawer after my demise.) My husband drives me to the airport full of random remarks about what a beautiful day it is for flying and be sure to tell my mother he enjoyed the candy. I, on the other hand, try to seize these precious moments to make it clear to him that "after I'm gone" I expect him to remarry, really *expect* him to. How *could* he manage—a widower with those five children? He makes a completely unsuccessful attempt to choke back his laughter and then pats me on the shoulder. "Honey, you're nuts," he says without a trace of sympathy. "But think of Will Rogers," I say plaintively, "and Wiley Post. And remember the Hindenburg." "Good heavens, that was a zeppelin," he says. Yeah, and a lot of difference that made.

By the time the plane is ready to depart I have been fortified with tranquilizers, dramamine, and intoxicating beverages. Nevertheless I creep up the entrance ramp a craven creature, escorted usually by the copilot, who recognizes a case of nerves when he sees one. "I suppose you've checked all the engines," I say, laughing wildly—giving a performance like James Cagney being led to the chair in one of those old Warner Brothers movies. The only reason I don't change my mind and make a break for it right down the ramp is because they have by this time absconded with my luggage, which is now, I presume, locked away in the hold.

I never bring reading material aboard a plane because I am convinced that if I'm not right there, alert every minute, keeping my eye on things, heaven knows what might happen to us. When it comes to selecting a seat I am torn between my wish to sit well back in the tail (surely the

safest place to be when we crash) and the feeling that it is my civic duty to take a place next to the window where I can keep a constant watch over the engines. You have no idea how heedless and selfish some passengers are—reading magazines and munching sandwiches the while that I, alone, am keeping that plane aloft by tugging upward on the arms of my chair and concentrating intensely, sometimes for hours. And when it becomes absolutely clear that something is amiss, who has to ask that simple, straightforward question that will clarify things? I do. Honestly, I don't think these people care whether they live or die.

On a recent daylight flight to Washington, D.C., I was quick to notice that in spite of the fact that the weather was brilliantly clear our plane kept losing altitude. By which I mean it was dropping and dropping and dropping. "Stewardess," I said, raising my voice to a whisper, "is something the matter?" She flashed me a wide, Cinemascope smile and said, "I'll ask the Captain, if you wish." By this time my stomach was in such a precarious condition that I didn't trust myself to vocalize, so I merely made a little gesture meaning "that would be very nice." She disappeared into the cockpit, where, evidently, the intercom between pilot and passengers had been left open. Presently we were all able to hear the stewardess reporting, "The passengers want to know if something is the matter." The next thing we heard was a short oath and a hoarse male voice saying, "The hell with the passengers, I'm up to my ears in trouble."

Well, talk about a conversation stopper. Even the jaunty junior executives who, a moment before, had been exchanging noisy jokes about an extremely co-operative girl named Mildred retreated into silence behind their copies of *The Wall Street Journal,* which could be seen to flap and rustle in their trembling hands. Mercifully, there were no more bulletins from the cabin and we landed uneventfully, none the worse for wear. Well, I can't speak for the other passengers, of course. But after five days' bed rest I felt fine.

I know perfectly well that people who talk about "their flights" are on a par, conversationally, with people who talk about their operations. Consequently at social gatherings I always try to find a subject that is genuinely interesting, like, for instance, my dishwasher. (The man was here *three* times and still the water pours out all over the kitchen floor.) However I barely get started when someone interrupts me to say, "Listen, do you want to hear a really hair-raising story?" And I know we are off on another saga of the perils of this age of flight. A songwriter recently told me that his plane from the Coast was barely aloft when he overheard the following exchange between a dear old lady across the aisle from him and the stewardess:

DEAR OLD LADY I hate to mention this, stewardess, but I think one of the engines is on fire.

STEWARDESS No, indeed, madam, those little sparks you see are part of the normal functioning. May I ask, is this your first flight?

DEAR OLD LADY That's right. My children gave me this
trip as a present for my eighty-sixth birthday.
STEWARDESS I thought so. Many of our first-time passengers are a little nervous, but there is nothing to worry
about. Not one member of the crew has had less than
two thousand hours in the air.
DEAR OLD LADY Thank you, my dear. I felt I was being
a little silly. But before you go would you mind taking
a look out my window here?
STEWARDESS Why, certainly. If it will make you feel a
little better I'll be glad to—*oh my God!*

The engine, needless to say, was on fire, but I won't
wear you out with all the details—except to say that all
landed safely, including the old lady, who was heard re-
marking to her son-in-law, "You won't believe this, Henry,
but *I* had to tell them the plane was on fire."

In every tale of air-borne trouble one hears the same
recurring phrase: "The passengers behaved so well." They
do, too. They are brave, considerate, prompt, reverent,

and, I sometimes think, just plain lacking in common sense. A friend of mine who is a theatrical agent told me that when her plane stopped at Gander an announcement came over the loudspeaker to the effect that there would be a six-hour delay for repairs. Twenty minutes later, to everybody's surprise, there was a second announcement asking the passengers to reboard the plane. Several of them buttonholed the pilot on the way up to the ramp and said, "I thought we were stopping for repairs." He smiled winningly and replied, "We changed our minds. We've decided to go on." And would you believe it, every single one of those passengers went back onto that plane. If it had been me, I'd have hitchhiked my way home, or taken a canoe. Listen, before I'd have put one foot on that plane I would have stayed right there and begun life anew in Gander.

Even in the very best weather I find it advisable to take dramamine, if for no other reason than it helps one to cope with the smiles of the personnel. Another thing that has to be coped with is the handy leaflet of information provided so thoughtfully by every airline.

A year ago my husband and I made our first overseas flight. During the endless delay in the London Airport it became clear that we had been assigned to the fifth section of what was originally intended as a three-section flight. Obviously they were out combing the hangars for something that would fly. I could imagine the arguments: "Oh, don't be such a worrywart. You put a little 3-in-1 Oil in her and she'll go up." I'll say this: they made no hurried, spot decisions, because it was seven hours later that we assembled on the runway to inspect the craft that was to be our home away from home on the North Atlantic. My husband took one look and said, "Good Lord, it's *The Spirit of St. Louis!*" Of course he was exaggerating, but there was no doubt it was an extremely elderly plane. A little paint and paper would have done wonders, though not, I feared, enough.

As we were poking our way to our seats, I heard the stewardess ask the pilot, "Did you ever see one like this, Bill?" I was spared his answer, because there was a loud *flap!* caused by two upper berths which had suddenly, and for no apparent reason, dropped down over our heads. These berths were never occupied (for what I'm sure were good and sufficient reasons) and, since they resisted the efforts of every single member of the crew to lock them, they kept appearing and disappearing with about the same frequency as the commercials on the Late, Late Show.

Eventually, or in a lot more time than it takes to tell about it, we were over the ocean. It was two o'clock in the morning, *my* time, but we were all eating scrambled eggs because, I gathered, it was now breakfast time in Scranton, Pennsylvania. I had become accustomed to the rhythm of this particular plane: it went shlumn-blip, shlumn-blip, which seemed perfectly reasonable to me. Soon, however, I began to detect what I assumed was an alien note in this refrain. Now it went shlumn-blip, shlumn-blip, *pickety*. It got worse in a moment when the upper berths began

45

once more to flop open, and with the addition of this new
leitmotiv we had what sounded like a full chorale: shlumn-
blip, shlumn-blip, pickety, *flap!* Feeling that I must dis-
tract myself, I hunted through the seat pocket for something to read. Imagine my horror when I fished out a
pamphlet entitled "Your Role in a Water Landing." The
minutes flew by like hours as I read on and on. Clearly
the world lost a great humorist when the author of this
piece went to write for the airlines. In his jaunty phrase,
the great North Atlantic—now looming menacingly below
us—became "the drink." "Should we go into the drink,"
he wrote, blithe as a skylark, "you should be none the
worse for the dunking." I was already the worse, just con-
templating the prospect. But let's get back to that title:
"Your Role in a Water Landing." Put it that way and I'm
simply not interested. I know my role in a water landing.
I'm just going to splash around and sob. What I want to
know, what I am really and truly curious about, is *their*
role in a water landing. But the author kept pretty mum
about that part of it. As for me, I kept entirely mum until
the moment, ten hours later, when I was able to kiss the
sweet soil of Idlewild.

Because I seem to be giving the entirely false impression
that anything that happens out of the routine, flightwise,
is apt to be harassing, I would like to conclude with a little
tale that should serve as proof that it is possible to have an
adventure in a plane that is merely amusing.

A businessman I know who toils in New York City had
to rush to Chicago to conclude an important business deal.

He sped out to La Guardia and was delighted to secure a seat on a jet bound for San Francisco that had a stopover in Chicago. He was almost there, and congratulating himself that the jet had saved him an hour in time, when word came back from the pilot that, due to fog conditions in Chicago, the plane was proceeding directly to San Francisco. Shortly afterward (these jets are swift), he found himself at the airport in San Francisco. After making a series of loud, intemperate remarks (by his own admission, he made a spectacle of himself), he struck up an acquaintance with a number of airline executives who were distressed, nay *distrait*, to discover his predicament. Heads rolled and red tape disappeared as though by magic as the management went into action. Within an hour they had bundled him onto the last precious seat of a jet bound for New York with a stopover in Chicago. Such are the wonders of jet speed that he found himself approaching Chicago before you could say Jack Robinson, and also before the fog had lifted. Naturally, the plane kept right on going to New York. I asked him what he said when once

more he landed at La Guardia, having flown from coast to coast and back without ever having seen Chicago. He replied, "I don't think I said anything. I just sat there on the bench and cried." But I don't really believe that. This man is forty-six years old and he weighs two hundred and ten pounds. I don't really think he would cry, out loud, in public—do you?

HOW TO TALK TO A MAN

Of course, I have no statistics, and nobody ever tells me anything. But I suspect one reason marriages break up is that some wives, after spending a full hour in rich, deeply shared silence with the beloved, are apt to remark, "In heaven's name, *say* something, will you?"

The problem stems quite naturally from the fact that women speak because they wish to speak, whereas a man speaks only when driven to speech by something outside himself—like, for instance, he can't find any clean socks, or he has just read in a headline that Herbert Hoover fore-

49

sees no depression in 1960. A wife who really feels cheerful and chatty early in the morning (a circumstance that can be explained only by a faulty metabolism) can always inveigle her husband into conversation by using a little imagination and by learning to snap up cues. She might say, "Speaking of clean socks reminds me, did you read John Hutchens' review of *The Mackerel Plaza?*" Now he's on the spot. He has to say something, even if it is only to comment on the total absence of any connection between his socks and *The Mackerel Plaza.*

I have a rather engaging little trick for stirring my own husband into statement. I just quote a few lines from the balcony scene of *Romeo and Juliet.*

"He speaks," I say in mock lyrical tones, "but he says nothing. What of that? His eye discourses. I will answer *it.*" Thus prodded, he is apt to say things he will have to retract later, but there are risks to everything.

Actually, if you had wanted a husband who would be a stimulating conversationalist, you should have married a mechanic or even a gardener—certainly not an author or a professional man or, last of all, a lecturer. When we got married, my husband was a lecturer and professor of drama and I used to imagine the stimulating, intellectual conversation we were going to have at breakfast. Like this:

ME   That play last night was interesting, didn't you think?

HIM   Very. Of course, the author is still heavily in debt to Chekhov—the despairing protagonist, the shackling environment, the complete stasis in the third act and, of course, the total absence of climax.

ME Yes, he has an almost kinetic sense of atmosphere, but he never licked the story line.

HIM Licked it? He should have joined it.

      (Appreciative chuckles all around.)

This, however, is a transcript of the actual conversation:

HIM (Despairingly) I'll bet this is diet bread.

ME What's the matter with diet bread?

HIM (After a pause) Everything. Why don't we eat things other people eat?

ME Such as—

HIM (Passionately) Those flat sticky things with jam inside them. Or muffins. Why don't we ever have muffins?

ME (Evenly) Very well, dear, we'll have muffins.

HIM (Suspiciously) Oh, I know you. You'll get diet muffins.

We really should have our own radio show.

It's interesting to observe the phenomenon that will cause a husband who hasn't opened his yap in weeks suddenly to find the gift of speech. Just order a new coat that differs in any way at all from the last five coats you have owned and watch Big Chief Still Waters blossom into Alistair Cooke, a veritable fount of articulation. "Yes, I know it's the new style, but we haven't got a space ship yet. Oh, I see, all the fullness in the back is *supposed* to make you look as if you're standing in a head wind! Well, never mind. It'll be economical, anyway—in the summer you can take it to the beach and use it as a cabana." Etc.

There is a cure for this. Just take him with you when

51

you go to Bonwit Teller's. Once you deposit him on that chaste Empire sofa in Misses' Suits, his whole attitude will change—not to mention his pulse, temperature, and rate of breathing. Precisely what causes men to go into shock in Bonwit's I can't imagine. My husband keeps looking from right to left in a state of ashen panic, as though he feared at any moment one of those elegant salesladies was going to snatch him and set his hair. But at any rate he brings a more judicious attitude to the subject of high style. "Yeah, yeah," he mutters at my first reappearance from the depths of the dressing room, "it looks great, let's get out of here."

Some men do most of their talking at the movies ("Good Lord, I knew I was in for *Moby Dick*, but you didn't say there was going to be forty minutes of cartoons!"). My father is a man like that. The most he has spoken in thirty years was on a certain unfortunate occasion when my mother (who can't remember the titles of movies) took him for the second time in three weeks to see Bob Hope in *Son of Paleface*.

But let's get down to cases:

How to Talk to a Man When He's Snoring

When I speak of snoring I do not refer to the simple, rhythmic snorp-bleet, snorp-bleet to which every loyal, understanding wife should adjust. I am here talking of snoring which has the range and crescendo of a musical composition—where you can actually detect a verse, two choruses, and a release. I used to give my husband a gen-

tle shove and whisper, "Honey, turn over—you're snoring." The result was that he turned over and in two minutes was snoring louder than before, while I lay awake for hours planning a separation and wondering what we were going to do about the children and all those monogrammed towels.

Then I learned the trick, which is to get the snorer interested. Don't make statements. Ask questions. Shake him and say, "Darling, what are you trying to say?" Eventually, after a few incoherent "huh, huhs" and "what, whats", he'll ask, "What do you mean, what am I trying to say?" After a few more equally pointless questions and answers he will be so cross that it will be at least fourteen minutes before he'll be able to snore again, giving you ample time to get to sleep first.

How to Talk to a Man in a Fashionable Restaurant

I once read an interview with the Duchess of Windsor in which she said that she and the Duke hated to eat in public restaurants because they had to converse so animatedly and affect such feverish interest in each other—lest rumors start that they were estranged—that she never could enjoy a bite of her dinner. It ought to be (but somehow it isn't) helpful to tell yourself that you're not the Duchess of Windsor and that nobody is even the tiniest bit interested in whether you and your husband have spoken since 1943. The point is that in a restaurant (like Sardi's, for instance) where you are surrounded by the tinkling laughter of beautiful models engaged in vivacious conversation with movie actors, you do feel somehow that you can't just sit there, specters at the feast, looking like two people who have just learned that their 1958 income-tax return was being investigated. Of course there are lots of things on your mind that you could say ("Well, you saw that Chris got D in Health Habits again," or, "The man came about the drier and he says we need a whole new unit"), but this doesn't seem to be the time or the place.

A couple I know have solved the problem beautifully. She just tells him the story of The Three Bears, a narrative which is admirable for the purpose because of its many rising inflections. And he helps her out by occasionally interjecting a remark like "By George, you mean she ate every last bite of the baby bear's porridge?" Do try it some time. Anybody overhearing you will conclude that you are

discussing a new television spectacular—either that, or you're both a little bit dotty. If you should be concerned about this aspect of the matter, or if you should happen to intercept a stunned glance from the waiter, you can always drop in a covering remark like "Red Buttons—*there's* your Baby Bear!"

How to Talk to a Man When He's Taking a Shower

Here you have a captive audience and an ideal opportunity to tell a husband a number of things that you don't want him to hear. (Later on you can say, "Of course I told you, you just don't listen!") There is no limit to the amount of unwelcome information you can get off your chest at one clip in these circumstances: "The man from Macy's was here and I took thirty dollars out of your wallet," and "Betty called, she and George are going to drop in," and

"The children are going to be in a Humpty-Dumpty play tonight—Col is playing Humpty and John is one of the king's men and we both have to go."

How to Talk to a Man on the Telephone, Long Distance

When a man calls you from Tulsa, he invariably makes the mistake of calling either from a public bar or from his mother's living room. Neither setting is exactly conducive to a free exchange of ideas. There, within earshot of his fellow revelers or his mother, he can hardly say the one thing you want to hear, which is that he misses you terribly, it's been a nightmare, a nightmare! and he's never going to make a trip alone again. For that matter, you can't tell him you miss him either, because the children are there with you and they become downright alarmed at any hint that their parents have preserved this degrading adolescent attachment so far into senility. So, if you're not careful, it's going to be a total loss of five dollars and eighty-five cents.

Don't, whatever you do, launch into that foolish litany of last-minute health bulletins: "Yes, I'm fine, yes, Chris is fine, yes, Gilbert is fine, etc." Let it be understood in advance that if one of the children should be rushed to the hospital for an emergency appendectomy, you'll mention it.

Use the time to clear up some matter that has really been troubling you. Explain that you finally saw *The Bridge on the River Kwai*, and that it was marvelous, marvelous, but you didn't understand the ending. Get him to

57

explain it. Did Alec Guinness mean to set off that dynamite or didn't he? What about William Holden? Who really killed him? This is important. When William Holden gets shot, a woman wants to know the facts. Later, when you hang up, you may discover that you've forgotten to ask what time his plane arrives at La Guardia, but the call won't have been a total loss.

How to Talk to a Man before a Party

There are two occasions when a wife absolutely expects that a loyal husband will cleave to her side: when she's having a baby and when she's having a party. (It's interesting to note that the announcements on both occasions always seem to imply that these are joint projects, but, when it comes right down to it, who has that baby and who has that party? You do.) No one expects a husband to go out in the kitchen and stuff eggs, but he might try being a moral support during that horrible, hollow half hour before the first guest arrives. There you are, wandering aimlessly about from ash tray to ash tray, suddenly as much a stranger in your own home as if you were on Person to Person showing Ed Murrow around. And one of the reasons you can't rely on your husband for a comforting remark is that this is precisely the moment he chooses to lay a few asphalt tiles on the floor of the rumpus room.

If you should stand on your rights and say, "Don't you disappear anywhere at all, just stay right here!" he will eventually lighten the tension by muttering, "Great Scott, you forgot limes!" What he should say, of course, is some-

58

thing soothing, like "Darling, you look charming in that dress. It reminds me of the night we met, do you remember? You were dancing with Hugh, and I came in with Connie and Leo . . ."

The last time we had a party I suggested this constructive line of conversation to my husband. He claimed that he'd once said something very similar, and what I said was "In heaven's name, stop chattering about the night we met and go get some ice."

How to Talk to a Man after You've Told Him That If He Doesn't Stop Fiddling with That Old Toaster He Is Going to Blow a Fuse, and He Does

There is no way. Just light a candle and count ten or your blessings, whichever is greater.

A CHILD'S GARDEN OF MANNERS

Have you noticed a strange thing about etiquette books?
They are all written for grown-ups. *Us.*

I really don't understand it. Most adults have lovely
manners; it's a pleasure to have them around. Ask an adult
to hand you your glasses and he says, "Here they are,
dear." He doesn't put them behind his back and say,
"Guess which hand?" And when you give him a birthday
present he doesn't burst into tears and say, "I already *have*
Chinese checkers!" What I wish is that Emily and Amy
and the others would get to work on the real trouble area
—people under twelve.

60

I know that small children have a certain animal magnetism. People kiss them a lot. But are they really in demand, socially? Are they sought after? Does anybody ever call them on the telephone and invite them to spend the weekend on Long Island? Do their very own grandmothers want them to spend the *whole* summer in Scranton? No. For one thing they bite, and then they keep trying to make forts with mashed potatoes. It holds them back, socially. If you have any doubt about the matter, ask yourself one question. When, by some accident, you find yourself at a large party with children present, do you just naturally gravitate over to that corner of the room where the little ones are playing Indian Spy under the card table? See what I mean? These kids need help—and direction.

Now, I'm the last one to be talking about manners. Just this week at a dinner party I let myself get rattled by the innocent question of a young man who was the son of my hostess and a freshman at Lehigh. All he wanted to know was whether I voted for Al Smith or Hoover in 1928. In the deep, troubled reverie produced by this line of questioning, I lost my head completely and consumed not only the entire salad of the man on my right but also one of his Parker House rolls. As I say, I'm not the one to write that book, *Tips for Tots*. But in the total absence of any definitive work on the subject, and inspired as I am by a passion for public service, I would like to make a few random suggestions:

Table Manners for Children

The first point to be established is that one does not sit *on* the table. One sits on the chair, and in such a way that all four legs touch the floor at the same time. (I am of course speaking of the four legs of the chair; children only *seem* to have four legs.) For children who will rock and tilt anyway, I suggest (a) built-in benches, (b) the practice of instilling in such children a sense of noblesse oblige, so that when they go crashing back onto their heads they go bravely and gallantly and without pulling the tablecloth, the dinner, and a full set of dishes with them. This last may sound severe, but it will be excellent training if they should ever enter the Marines, or even Schrafft's.

We don't have to bother about little niceties such as which fork is the shrimp fork (at these prices, who is giving them shrimp?). We will suppose, and safely, that the child has only one fork. If this child is interested in good manners and/or the sanity of his parents, he will not use the fork to (a) comb his hair, (b) punch holes in the tablecloth, or (c) remove buttons from his jacket. Nor will he ever, under any circumstances, place the tines of the fork under a full glass of milk and beat on the handle with a spoon.

So far as the food itself is concerned, it would be well for the child to adopt a philosophical attitude about that dreary procession of well-balanced meals by reminding himself that in eighteen years or less he will be free to have frozen pizza pies and fig bars every single night. And he should remember, too, that there is a right way and a wrong way to talk about broccoli. Instead of the gloomy mutter, "Oh, broccoli again—ugh!" how much better the cheery "I guess I'll eat this broccoli first and get it over with."

Finally, children should be made to understand that no matter how repellent they find a given vegetable, they may not stuff large handfuls of it into their pockets, particularly if the vegetable is creamed. This sorry but unfortunately common practice not only deprives the child of necessary vitamins but frequently exposes him to intemperate criticism and even physical violence.

Behavior at the Theater or Movies

Children should not bring guns or slingshots or cats to the theater. And for other reasons they shouldn't bring hats or gloves or rubbers—unless you have the time to go back to the theater and pick them all up afterward.

It is always worth while to give them exact change (thirty cents for the movie, five cents for candy), especially if the movie is going to be *The Son of the Monster*. Suspense has the curious effect on many children of causing them to swallow nickels.

The mannerly child will decide once and for all whether he wishes to sit on the seat pulled down (like old people) or whether he wants to sit high on the edge in the "up" position. Once he has made up his mind, he will not vacillate between the two positions, or he will very likely be thrown out onto the street by the ushers.

If children are going to eat at the movies, and they are,

63

they should be encouraged to buy candy that doesn't roll. Sour balls roll. And the fallout from a ten-cent box of sour balls is considerably greater than from a five-cent box. If you have any interest in making a host of new acquaintances all at once, there is no better way than to escort a pair of five-year-old twins to the movies and present each of them with a large box of sour balls. With the sense of timing that is innate in even the youngest children, they wait until the main feature starts before dropping both boxes on the floor. And then they're *off*, scrambling on hands and knees, down under the seats through a forest of legs, foraging, retrieving, sobbing. And for six rows in every direction wild-eyed patrons are leaping to their feet and splitting the air with questions: "In heaven's name, what are you *doing* down there? Will you get out? Where do you belong? Where is your mother?" etc. For this reason I suggest chocolate bars. It will ruin their clothes and spoil their dinner but that can't be helped.

Rules of Peaceful Coexistence with Other Children

Children should eschew violence, by which I mean that they should not hit each other on the head with ice skates or telephones or geography books. It ought to go without saying that polite children never push each other down the stairs, but I'm not sure that it does. Karen, my four-year-old niece, recently pushed her baby sister down the back stairs. After her mother had rescued the victim, she flew at the oppressor and shouted, "What's the matter with you? You can't push Joanie down the stairs!" Karen listened carefully, all innocence and interest, and finally said, "I can't? How come?"

Parenthetical note to parents: in trying to keep older children from doing permanent physical damage to their juniors, it is probably not advisable to adopt the tit-for-tat type of punishment ("If you pull Billy's hair again, I'm going to pull *your* hair!"). This method would appear to have a certain Old Testament rightness about it, but the danger is that you may put yourself into a position where you will be forced into massive retaliation. And, when it comes right down to it, you can't really punch that kid straight in the eye or spit in his milk. Personally, I'm in favor of generalized threats like "If you make that baby cry once more I swear I'll clip you." In this instance the word "clip" is open to a variety of interpretations and leaves you more or less free to inflict such punishment as you are up to at the moment.

Respect for the Feelings of Others

One of the reasons children are such duds socially is that they say things like "When do you think you're going to be dead, Grandma?" We're all going to be dead, of course, but nobody wants to be put on the spot like that.

It is not to be expected that a small child can be taught never to make a personal remark. But there is a time and a place. For instance, the moment Mommy is all dressed up in her new blue chiffon and doesn't look a day older than twenty-five, well, twenty-eight, is *not* the time for Gilbert

66

to ask, "Why do you have all those stripes on your fore-head, Mommy?"

Children should realize that parents are emotionally in-secure, and that there are times when they need loving kindness. Unfortunately, a relationship with a child, like any love affair, is complicated by the fact that the two parties almost never feel the same amount of ardor at the same time. One blows hot while the other blows cold, and vice versa. On the day you're flying to Athens (for two whole weeks) and you're already frantic with concern and full of terrible forebodings that you will never see the little lambs again, you can hardly round them up to say good-by. And when you do locate one of them, he scarcely looks up from his work. "Darling," you say, "aren't you go-ing to say good-by and give me a *good* kiss? I'm going to be gone for two whole weeks." "Sure," he says, "'bye, Mom, can I have a Coke?"

Of course he too has moments when affection swells—the wrong moments. First he reduces you to babbling incoherence by (a) climbing in the kitchen window and smashing three geraniums, (b) taking the mail from the mailman and dropping half of it in a puddle, (c) spilling a bottle of navy-blue suede dressing on the cat. Then, as you are pouring Merthiolate on your scratches—incurred while cleaning up the cat—he returns covered with mud, having just buried a squirrel. You are deep in philosophical speculation centering around the miraculous fact that this child was not adopted (at least you don't have to fight the temptation to send him back). And naturally, it's right at this moment that he takes it into his head to give you one of his Jack-the-Ripper hugs, curling muddy cowboy boots around your knees and plastering you with sandy kisses.

Respect for the Property of Others

Children should bear in mind that, no matter how foolish it seems, adults become attached to material objects, like typewriters, wrist watches, and car keys. I admit that I am once again working without statistics, but I do have the feeling we wouldn't have so many disturbed parents in this country if children could be made aware of the unwisdom of using their fathers' best fountain pens to punch holes in evaporated milk cans. (If you're interested, there is one foolproof way of holding onto pens and pencils: you hire a man with a gun to sit by the desk all day, and then you or your husband or some other responsible adult takes the night shift.)

Just as there are animals that kill prey they have no intention of eating, so are there children who take things they have no way of using. It may be reprehensible, but it is at least understandable that a child should take a sterling-silver gravy ladle to the beach; it's almost as good to dig with as a sand shovel. But why do they take the little knobs off the tops of lamp shades, or meat thermometers, or the dialing wheels off the television set? Sometimes when you investigate what seems to be meaningless mayhem, you find that there is a certain idiotic logic behind the whole thing: when I found one of the smaller boys unfurling a roll of toilet paper out of the attic window, it turned out that he was merely trying to discover how long a roll of toilet paper really was. I can understand that, sort of. But I never did understand why he cut the bows off my blue suede shoes.

Children have such a lively sense of the inviolability of what belongs to them (as you've noticed if you ever tried to throw out an old coloring book) that it should be easy for them to remember that adults, too, have little fetishes about their personal possessions ("You don't like anybody to play with your tractor, do you? Well, Daddy doesn't like anybody to play with his tape recorder.").

Sometimes it's hard to know just what to say. Last winter I found on the breakfast table a letter addressed to Mommy Kerr. It was on my very best stationery, and there were ten brand-new four-cent stamps plastered all over the envelope. When I pulled out the letter, the message read:

> *Dear Mommy,*
> *John is mad at you becuase you won't let us put our snowballs in the freeser but I am not mad at you becuase I love you*
>
> *Your Frend, Colin*

Well, there you are. When you get right down to it, it was worth forty cents.

AS I WAS SAYING
TO MRS. ROCKEFELLER
The Confessions of a Status Finder

I have just finished reading The Status Seekers *and now* I'm really upset. Here I've been, all these years, supposing that I was a perfect example of a low-status type. Oh, I just *knew*, that's all. In fact, there didn't seem to be any other possibility. Here we were: Democrats, driving around in a ten-year-old Chevy, eating meat loaf, and going to see *American* movies. Little things, you say, but they add up—particularly when you have five children and not one of them can spell.

But I wasn't really worried. I was bearing up nicely until I read Vance Packard's book. And the reason I am at sixes and sevens now is because it seems, and you won't believe this, it seems that I am really a high-status type. But here's the terrible thing: nobody knows it. My friends (a low-status group if I ever saw one) don't know it. The salesgirls in Saks Fifth Avenue clearly don't know it. My very own mother doesn't know it or she wouldn't keep saying to me, "For heaven's sake, buy yourself a decent set of dishes." This is simply not the remark one makes to a high-status person.

Oh, I am surrounded by skeptics, but I refer them all to Mr. Packard. He says very plainly that "women who are really secure in their upper-class status may become fond of a good outfit and wear it for years." You'll know how secure I am when I tell you that I still have this suit I bought before I was married. (It's a little tight now, so I just don't button the last three buttons.) But fond of it? If I weren't afraid of sounding mawkish, I'd come right out and say that I'm just plain crazy about that brown tweed suit. It may be fifteen years old this month, but it's just as baggy as the day I bought it. And it's suitable for so many occasions. Whether I am taking two sick cats to the vet, spreading peat moss on the rose bushes, or merely staining the front door, I know I'm dressed correctly when I'm wearing that suit.

There are those who may scoff to read Mr. Packard's

report that "the fabulously well-dressed Mrs. Winston Guest recently took with her to Europe a suit she has been wearing for eight years." Now it seems perfectly clear to me why Mrs. Guest took that suit to Europe. It's probably been hanging there getting on her nerves for seven years. By this time she's ashamed to give it to the help and reluctant to burn it. So what could be simpler than shoving it through a porthole? If I ever go to Europe again, that's exactly what I mean to do with this horrible brown tweed suit. Okay, I lied when I said I was crazy about it.

But let's get back to the facts. Another dead giveaway of my high social status is the way I entertain. Mr. Packard insists that at the upper-class level people "tend to prefer relaxed informality. Food typically is offered casually. There may be amiable and fairly open flirting and talking. Weaving figures may offer toasts." Honestly, if I didn't know better I'd swear that Packard was here one night last week. But then I imagine he has his spies, don't you?

As for this business about food being offered casually, I've actually been known to say, "Bill, I think you'll find pretzels on the second shelf." How could you be more upper-status than that? Mr. Packard concludes his summary of entertaining among the elect by stating flatly that "the people having the party at the upper level usually are not trying to prove anything. Publicity in the newspapers is not sought." Well, I should think not. With those weaving figures offering toasts, it seems to me the less said about the whole thing the better. But isn't it nice to know that when you are not trying to prove anything with a party

74

you are *really* proving that you are a high-status person?

Reading further (you notice how this is all adding up, don't you?), we learn that "the slim figure is more of a preoccupation with women of the upper classes. As you go down the scale, married women take plumpness more calmly." Observe that there is nowhere the suggestion that the upper-class female may not be plump. No, the implication is clear. It's all right to be plump as long as you're not calm about it.

Well, as far as that goes, you should have seen me trying on bathing suits in Lane Bryant's last summer. Not that there was any chance you'd have seen me, since I wouldn't even allow the motherly saleswoman to witness the struggles of that dreadful half hour. I tried on suit after suit, all of them designed by some shut-in in California who,

it seems to me, would benefit from a beginner's course in anatomy. But at each succeeding glimpse of myself in the rearview mirror I burst into wild outcries and muffled sobs. Indeed, I was anything but calm as I went off to soothe myself with a butterscotch sundae.

And don't worry about the quality of your conversation. Once you begin to get the hang of it you will find yourself just naturally making statements that are irreproachably upper-status. For instance, should the occasion arise, you might say, "Gimme a hunk ['the high-status person uses unpretentious language'] of that pumpernickel" ["only the upper classes like firm, hard bread"]. If you want to be really on the safe side, you might add, parenthetically, "but make it a small hunk," which would indicate that you were not taking plumpness calmly. As I say, it's a technique that can be learned. What's nice for me is that I was *born* liking pumpernickel bread.

Now that I've laid out the evidence and proved beyond question that I am a true high-status type, there is one statement in the book that comes back to haunt me. It says, "Medical investigators have noticed as you get near the bottom of the social scale, there is an abrupt rise in a disorder called anomie—feeling isolated, loosely attached to the world, and convinced that things are tough all over."

Feeling isolated? Loosely attached to the world? Convinced that things are tough all over? But that's the way *I* feel. That's the way I feel all the time. Now what do I do, Mr. Packard?

CAN THIS ROMANCE BE SAVED?
Lolita and Humbert Consult a Marriage Counselor

It was a mistake to read Vladimir Nabokov's Lolita *and the* Ladies' Home Journal *on the same evening. The total effect was a little confusing.*

The counselor interviews Humbert, and reports his side of the story:

Humbert was a tall, graying man. The natural pallor of his skin was perhaps accentuated by the drabness of his present garb. With his quiet, old-world charm he made me welcome in the cell and spoke quite readily of his broken romance.

"Doctor, picture—if you will—my darling, my nymphet, my Lolita, her scrawny, brown, twelve-year-old legs splashed all over with daubs of Mercurochrome, which spread like roses under the little white wings of Band-aids.

"To watch her sit at the kitchen table and play jacks was to know what Aristotle meant by pity and terror and to feel with Oedipus, arriving blind and gutted at Colonus. The jacks, in her grubby paws, flew into the air like little prisms of silver, like stars. And when sometimes it happened, as often it did, that the small rubber ball dropped from her hands into the butter dish (my darling was not very well co-ordinated), the stream of four-letter words that poured from her adorable mouth would have dazzled a fishmonger.

"Ah, Lolita—the snap, snap, splat of her bubble gum (she chewed twelve hours a day, my lamb did) will echo down the corridors of all my dreams. Even in Hell (*is* there a Hell, shall we talk theology, Doctor?) I will be bedeviled (forgive the pun; it was intended) by visions of the precious one who curled up so sweetly in my lap after I gave her five dollars.

"My conscience, that wary censor, that watchdog of memory, permits me to recall only the happy hours, when Lolita lay at my feet poring over movie magazines and munching candied apples (alas, she often brought these —the apples—to bed). Her bright eyes sparkled as she

gorged herself on pictures of pulchritudinous Rock or Tab
or Guy (surely I invent these names) here photographed
in a limed-oak study, there caught spread-armed and god-
like on a surfboard.

"It has been suggested that after her mother's
most timely demise I forced my attentions on this angel-
nymphet. (Idle roomers beget idle rumors.) But I swear to
you that I did no more than kidnap her from that summer
camp, right under the toothy smiles of the lady counselors
(fat, middle-aged sows, all of them, twenty-two or older).
It was little Lolita, accomplished beyond her years, who
seduced poor old Humbert. It was the fly, if you will, who
gobbled up the spider. You must remember that I was worn
down from poring over scholarly journals (did you know,

dear Doctor, that Dante's Beatrice was a nymphet of thirteen?) and weakened by the atrociously poor food provided by the series of mental institutions to which I was
periodically committed. On the other hand, my little lamb
chop was in fighting trim, lean and lithe from playing hop-
scotch. Oh, Lolita, oh those nights, *mon Dieu!* (that's
French, Doctor; I'm a very educated fellow).

"Imagine my horror when my darling, who—what is the
vulgar phrase?—who had it made, who had handsome,
hairy Humbert in the palm of her tiny hand, left,
scrammed, vamoosed, ran off. And ran off, would you believe it, with the first fat, balding slob who promised her a
glimpse of Hamburger Heaven. And I, all alone, bewailed
my outcast state and troubled the deaf deities with my
burping, noisy grief. Ah, laugh if you will, but hath not a
pervert eyes, hands, senses, passions, and affections? Do
you wonder that I killed him?

"And here I am, behind bars which contain me and en-
close me like my own parentheses. Yesterday and yesterday and yesterday I was always her victim, Doctor. An
unlikely story, you say, and yet you may have observed
how it sells."

The counselor interviews Lolita, and reports her *side of
the story:*

I would not say that my first interview with twelve-
year-old Lolita was entirely successful. In the first place,
she was busy manipulating her Yo-yo and seemed reluc-

tant to talk. After I had gained her confidence, she opened up a little.

"Look, Doc, it was a nightmare from the beginning. The night he swiped me from that camp and took me to the motel, do you know what he did to me? First of all, you've gotta get the picture that there's nothing in this room but the double bed and one bureau. So what happens? Humbert takes the three big drawers for his stuff and leaves me with those two little tiny drawers on top. I couldn't even get all my hair ribbons in. Was I burned up?

"I'll say this. He could be sweet enough when he wanted to. But as soon as we got out of bed in the morning, my troubles began. Boy did he overwork the togetherness bit. All this jazz about 'sharing' nearly drove me out of my little pink mind. If I went out on the front sidewalk to skip rope, *he* had to skip rope. We had to cut down the clothesline to get a rope big enough for him. Boy, you should

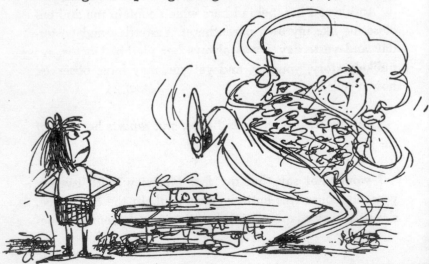

have seen him, huffing and puffing and getting his big clod-hoppers all tangled up in the rope. If I had an onion sandwich, you bet your life Big Daddy had to have an onion sandwich. He'd pile on the onions and then, as soon as he got it all down, he'd turn absolutely green and have to drink *gallons* of Bromo-Seltzer. All this time he'd be groaning and saying, 'You see, mah puhteet, I'd do any-thing for you—anything.' I'd come right out and tell him, 'Look, Pops, if you wanna do me a real favor, go to the movies and leave me alone for two hours.' Then he'd start to cry and say I was just trying to get rid of him. That guy cried so much he should have had windshield wipers for those glasses.

"But the worst of all was the way he hogged things. On Sunday morning, who used to toddle out in his pajamas and grab all the funnies first? Mr. Serutan. Of course by the time I got hold of them, they were an absolute mess. He used to pretend that he just wanted to know what I was reading. But he didn't fool me. A forty-year-old yak-king it up over Joe Palooka—I ask you. If you want the inside story, Doc, I'm looking for a more mature man."

The counselor gives his advice:

At first glance it seemed as though these two people were poles apart. To begin with, there was the vast differ-ence in their ages. Obviously it was difficult for an experi-enced girl like Lolita to put up with Humbert's childish-ness.

However, as our interviews continued, I was quick to

notice that they had a number of important things in common. For instance, Humbert, as a child, suffered from an "absent" mother. That is to say, his mother died when he was eighteen months old, and so, quite naturally, he hated her. As counselor, I was able to show Humbert that his rebellious attitude stemmed in large part from the fact that, as a child, he lacked that symbol of sensual pleasure, the cookie jar. Resentful at being abandoned by his mother, he was trying to penalize all other women who, in his fantasies, became "cookies." Humbert was quick to acknowledge the truth of my diagnosis. "Doctor," he said, "that's a new one on me."

Lolita, on the other hand, had a "present" mother who danced attendance on her night and day. Naturally she hated her. The mother, with that obtuseness so often found among females of the lower middle classes, made a fetish of propriety. Consequently she was unsympathetic to twelve-year-old Lolita's valiant efforts to form a sexual alliance with an older man. And, what was worse, she constantly interfered with Lolita's natural development by saying things like "Don't leave the soap in the bathtub" or "Get your fingers out of the plate." Is it any wonder that Lolita has spent her whole life trying to get her fingers in the plate?

The solution for this pair did not come all at once. But as our sessions drew to a close I felt that the future looked brighter for both of them. Lolita has agreed to stop bringing candied apples to bed. (The onion sandwiches are no longer a problem; since Lolita's gall bladder operation she is no longer able to tolerate raw onions.)

On his side, Humbert has agreed to stay in prison. With time off for good behavior, he can look forward to a parole in forty-five years. At this time he will be eighty-five and should be sufficiently mature to shoulder his responsibilities. Lolita will wait. (I have decided to take her into my home as a ward.) In the meantime, she is optimistic. As she herself expressed it, "With my luck, he'll *get* out of the clink."

Good luck to you both, Lolita and Humbert.

TALES OUT OF SCHOOL:
The Sandwich Crisis

I hear the most disquieting rumors that our school system is going from pot to worse and that all over America there are twelve-year-old boys who write seperate and Filladelphia and think an hypotenuse is a baby hippo. I gather it's a scandal, an absolute scandal. And if I don't seem properly irate about the whole matter, it's because I'm so grateful to schools.

I mean, think of those teachers keeping forty or fifty small children interested and occupied for five hours a day.

Well, maybe they're not interested and maybe they're not occupied, but the point is they're *there*. They're not in the kitchen making flour paste or in the living room carefully writing their initials on the coffee table.

It's considerations like these that make me perfectly willing to find out what an hypotenuse is and tell them. I can do that all right, and I can do homework—up to but not including long division. What I can't seem to do is pack a school lunch.

To begin with, I always pack lunches the night before, because in the early morning I can't remember how many children I have and naturally go wildly wrong on the number of sandwiches. At one o'clock in the morning I am in full possession of my faculties.

What I am not in possession of is something to make a sandwich with, unless you count that jar of what I *think* is apple butter and which I know we brought with us when we moved from New Rochelle.

I lean on the refrigerator door for twenty minutes and stare at the unlovely interior as though it were Playhouse 90. Meanwhile all the events of the past six months swim before me. There is not an item on the crowded shelves that isn't rich with bittersweet memories. There are five quart jars of mayonnaise that evidently were on sale sometime or other. There are no fewer than six plastic "space savers" (now empty), and no wonder there's no space in that icebox. There are two half bottles of club soda, improperly capped, and a sinister-looking turkey carcass that must have been there since Christmas (it *can't* have been

88

there since Thanksgiving). There are also a couple of cans of evaporated milk which they say you can keep in the cupboard, but I don't know that I believe that. After all, it's milk, isn't it?

Another woman could make a tasty sandwich spread by mixing evaporated milk and mayonnaise with some curry powder. But I lack the dash for this kind of experimentation. For that matter I lack the curry powder, and —what is more to the point—I lack qualities of leadership. Yes, I do. I'm an unfit mother and a rotten housekeeper, as shiftless and improvident as a character out of *God's Little Acre.*

What lends particular poignance to this moment is the fact that I was in a large chain store that very afternoon and could easily have bought some spiced ham. Of course I didn't actually see any spiced ham when I bought those nylon stockings, a philodendron plant, and two long-playing records, but surely they had some tucked away someplace. I know what I'm going to do for lunches next week, and there's no use talking me out of it. I'm going to go to a delicatessen on Monday afternoon and buy five quarts of lobster salad and some baked Virginia ham. Of *course* it will be expensive and we will have to economize on dinner all week by having canned chili and baked beans, but it will be worth it.

But to get back to this moment. Let's say, just for the sake of argument, that I find something to put in the sandwiches. (There's always that can of plovers' eggs somebody gave us as a joke last Easter.) The next problem is

89

to find something to put the sandwiches in. I know you can buy sandwich bags, but I never feel right about that when, after all, they give you all those nice little brown bags free with lettuce and bananas. But try and find a little brown bag at one o'clock in the morning. I usually wind up packing a sandwich, an apple, and two cookies in a bag that formerly held a twenty-six-pound turkey. Even after I tear off the top half of the bag and fold it down, it still looks as if it contained a painter's overalls.

Now there's the little item of milk money. In the school our children attend milk costs eight cents. Four children times four bottles of milk should give you a figure of thirty-two cents, or one quarter, one nickel, and two pennies. Break it down that way and one could just possibly locate thirty-two cents. In theory, the oldest boy could take the money and pay for the four bottles of milk when all assemble in the lunchroom. In practice, I have only to mention this eminently sensible plan to uncork such tears and lamentations from the other three as haven't been heard since the time I gave that large empty crate to the trashman, not knowing it was a clubhouse.

I don't know whether the others are ashamed to be seen with Chris in the lunchroom because his shirttail is always out, or whether they are afraid that he will skip town with the thirty-two cents. All I know is that I have to find four nickels and twelve pennies, which means rifling through all my summer purses, which are now in the attic. This is further complicated on days when Col needs fifteen cents for a box of crayons and Gilbert needs thirty-five cents for a new speller. I'll be glad when they raise the price of milk to ten cents. After all, they're entitled to a profit like everybody else, and dimes—you can find dimes.

Another item that will have to be prepared while the children sleep (along with the lunches) is a note to Johnny's teacher explaining just precisely what ailed him when he was absent from school last Tuesday, Wednesday, and Thursday. This will be complicated by the fact that I don't remember his teacher's name (Sister Mary Arthur was his teacher last year, but that's no help) and I will have to address the note "Dear Teacher," which reveals not only that I am woefully out of touch with my son but clearly without even the most rudimentary interest in the fine young woman who is molding his character. The next thing is that I haven't the least idea what ailed him last Tuesday. His eyes were glassy and he was burn-

ing up, just burning up, but I couldn't call the doctor because he didn't have a rash.

If the children are going to be sick anyway, I am always relieved to see spots. Anybody knows that you are within your rights to call a doctor if there's a rash. If, however, you are heedless enough to call the doctor just because your child has a temperature of 104 and you're frantic about him, you face the possibility that by the time the doctor arrives, a day after he's been called, the invalid will have a perfectly normal temperature and will be calmly engaged in making a tepee out of the bedclothes. The doctor may be perfectly polite (just keep him in bed for forty-eight hours) but he knows, and you know, that you're an idiot and a hysteric who thinks nothing of taking up a doctor's valuable time while all over the community genuine cases of chicken pox wait unattended.

But I am still left with that note to the teacher. And since I honestly don't know what blight was upon that boy, I will have to select an illness more or less out of the blue. This involves a nice balance of tone. Anything too casual suggests that I kept him home on a mere idle whim, perhaps to polish the silver. On the other hand I don't want to raise alarums by pretending that he was at death's door with diphtheria, which he is even now prepared to spread through the whole fourth grade. I usually settle for "stomach virus." That seems decently incapacitating without being too worrisome. I mean, anything in the stomach seems private and contained and wouldn't appear to invite the scrutiny of the Public Health Department.

Once I have the note and the milk money and lunches, I have only to locate hats, jackets, rubbers, schoolbooks and underpants. Now, I buy underpants the way some people buy gin—recklessly, extravagantly—and I secrete them at various key points throughout the house. As a result, I can always find eleven clean pairs of underpants in size eight. Of course there won't be a single pair in size four or size twelve, which means that I will have to go wash out three pairs, just exactly like those feckless, unthinking mothers who never buy underpants.

I know it's an admission of failure to say that I have to set out the boys' clothes for them. I understand that in well-regulated households the children perform these little services for themselves. Indeed I have heard, though I won't say that I believe it, that in various parts of this country there are nine-month-old infants who rinse out their own diapers.

What remarkable mothers these wee ones must have! I stand behind them every inch of the way. The only reason

I don't make our boys get everything ready for the morning is that I have sensitive eardrums and, in the morning, a nervous stomach, and I find that I tend to become un-hinged by the sobs of the doomed as they race up and down the stairs at a quarter to nine, hunting for left shoes and right mittens while announcing to the empty air, "I'm gonna be late and Sister'll *kill* me!"

To avoid this kind of thing and start the day sane, I do the amount of planning and co-ordinating that would be involved in landing two battalions in North Africa. So what happens? All four fly out the door, blessed silence descends —and then I look up to see Colin, who is inexplicably back and shouting frantically, "Quick, quick, the bus is wait-ing! I have to have an empty tomato can, eighteen inches of silver foil, and some Scotch tape. I'm making a lamp!"

One solution would be to tutor them all at home, but I think that's illegal. In any case, it's impossible. If Colin didn't go to school, *I'd* have to show him how to make a lamp.

95

OUT OF TOWN WITH A SHOW
Or What to Do until the Psychiatrist Comes

I used to love to go out of town with a show—you miss so
much at home. Oh, the exhilaration of being in Philadelphia just as the air is turning nippy, and knowing that
somebody else back in Larchmont will have to find the
storm windows. Indeed when I was younger and still in
love with room service, I felt, like any other red-blooded
American housewife, that a whole day spent rewriting the
first act was a small price to pay for the privilege of having

somebody else make my breakfast and bring it up to me on a tray. I don't know just when the truth caught up with me. But I have noticed recently that the mere thought of going to Boston with a musical causes me to tremble and drop small objects.

Many people have asked me—well, my father has asked me several times—why playwrights have to take a show out of town to try it out. Can't they tell anything from rehearsals?

The truth is that the playwright learns a great deal from rehearsals. He learns that the play is brave, haunting, luminous, tender, and hilarious, and that a cardboard container of coffee sent in from the delicatessen costs thirty cents. Everybody tells him how great the play is—the producer's secretary, the press agent's wife, the leading lady's mother. In fact, after spending only twenty minutes peering at a rehearsal from the back of an empty theater, they are so choked up with the magic of it all that they can barely vocalize. They squeeze the author's trembling hand and mutter hoarsely, "This is it, Sam—it can't miss." Not wishing to dispel the universal euphoria, Sam dismisses as unlikely his own secret theory that the play was badly cast, is being badly directed, and may have been badly written. Soon he is making discreet inquiries as to when the balloting closes for the Pulitzer Prize, and finally he comes home to tell his wife, "Honey, I don't see how it can miss."

And that's why he goes to Philadelphia: so he can see how it can miss.

Out of town the first thing he is up against is Murphy's Law. In Abe Burrows' definition, Murphy's Law states simply: if something *can* go wrong, it will. Now you wouldn't think it to look at me, but I just happen to be the world's expert on the things that can go wrong out of town. That's why I've taken up finger painting. The doctor says it will help me to forget. But while I can still remember, I would like to point out a few of the simpler rules for survival, for those of you who may be thinking of writing a play. And it's no use pretending that you have no intention of writing a play. There are distraught playwrights locked away in the Touraine Hotel this minute who, as recently as last year, were decently and profitably employed by Young and Rubicam or the Chock Full o' Nuts Company.

Learn to Cope with Room Service

We will start with the idea that the play will have to be entirely rewritten (there is no other possibility). This means that you will have to spend twenty-two hours out of every day closeted in a small hotel room with a rented typewriter and a very bad reproduction of a Utrillo.

Entombed as he is, the playwright usually makes the foolish mistake of supposing that he can count on room service to sustain the slender thread of life. This is patently ridiculous, as anyone who has ever waited three hours for two pots of black coffee will know. The thing to do is to bring along a couple of Care packages, or even a tin of biscuits. This will eliminate that air of panic which brings out the beast in room service, and will allow you to order

98

with the proper air of detachment. With any luck, you may stun the girl on the other end of the wire into instant action. A good method is to begin by asking her what day it is. Greet the news that it is Thursday with real appreciation. Then say, in an offhand, casual way, "Thursday, eh? Well, look, sometime over the weekend send me up a chicken sandwich, but there's no rush, I won't be checking out until the end of the month." Sometimes you'll get it in ten minutes.

The worst possible thing you can do, however, is to throw yourself on her mercy and suggest that you are dying of starvation. I know one playwright who swears he could have fixed that play if he hadn't spent all his time calling to inquire what had happened to his breakfast. And a pitiful sight he was, too—a large man of fifty-four shrieking into the telephone, "Yeah, yeah, yeah—I'm the scrambled eggs in 412!" Many writers of comedies exhaust their best energies composing humorous insults to hurl at room service (one I know went so far as to send a large funeral wreath to the kitchen "in memory of all those who have passed away in the last twenty-four hours"). I've never been up to anything so daring or original. I'm not the rugged type, and in the total absence of food, sleep, and clean laundry I tend to sink into childish incoherence. I take the phone in faltering hand and say, with what I assume in my enfeebled state to be dignity, "Hello, Room Service, is this Room Service—well, you're the *worst Room Service I ever met!*"

I know one hotel in Philadephia (name supplied on re-

99

quest) in which there is only one possible way to get room service. If you take off all your clothes, climb into the shower, and begin to lather, the boy will start banging on the door with your tray. You will go through a great many bath towels in this way, which will lead to further quarreling with the maid, but at least you'll get something to eat.

Stay out of the Lobby

Most authors waste a great deal of valuable energy slinking about the lobby during intermissions in a foolish effort to overhear the comments of the paying customers. They do this, mind you, even on those occasions when the audience has coughed and muttered throughout the entire first act with an animosity that has caused the actors to fear for their safety and the producer to leave town.

Even in these circumstances the playwright somehow imagines that he will overhear a tall, distinguished man (clearly a United States Senator) say to his companion, "Egad, Helen, it's plays like this that make theatergoing worth while."

Alas, this never happens. The people who attend the theater in tryout towns do not seem to recognize their obligation to discuss what they have just seen. Indeed, there is something downright perverse in the way they persist in believing that they are free to chat about their own affairs. Should you rub shoulders with a vivacious group out on the sidewalk, all you'll hear is a lady saying, "That's Jim for you, he *will* drink manhattans when he knows how I hate to drive the station wagon."

When I was in Philadelphia four years ago with a comedy called *King of Hearts*, I brushed so close to so many strangers that it's a wonder I wasn't arrested for soliciting. However, in two weeks of eavesdropping I only heard one remark that was in any way relevant to the show. This happened when a lady got up after the first act with dismay written all over her perplexed face. She turned to her husband and said plaintively, "George, this *can't* be *Dial M for Murder!*"

Even this wasn't as devastating as the experience a friend of mine had in Wilmington. It was opening night of his new melodrama, and after the second act he flew to his lookout in the lobby, where he was rewarded by hearing two couples actually discussing the play. "Well, Bill," asked the first man, "how do you like it?" My friend held his breath. Bill's answer was not long in coming. "You'd better ask Grace," he said; "she stayed awake."

Another reason authors should stay out of the lobby is that they look so terrible. Our playwright friend Sam, who is normally so natty that he has actually posed for a vodka advertisement, will turn up in the Shubert lobby in Philadelphia looking as unshaven, unkempt, and unstrung as the end man in a police lineup. In this condition he will strike terror into the hearts of the visiting investors, who will conclude that he is not likely to live long enough to finish the rewrite. He will also come under the inspection of some acquaintance who will take the trouble to write to his poor old mother and announce, "Sam is hitting the bottle again, or else he's got hepatitis."

Last season I spent three weeks in Boston with a musical, and of course went rapidly to seed. Now, a certain random, helter-skelter look is absolutely native to me. But on this occasion I sank into a really spectacular state of disrepair. I looked like a wire-service photo that would go nicely under the caption *She Survived Death March*. Dear friends would take me aside and say, "I know all about the second act, but you do have a comb, don't you?" In any case it was clear that in my derelict condition I couldn't be seen moping about the lobby, so I used to stand behind a pillar that was additionally sheltered by a large palm. It was in this retreat that I was accosted one night by a young man I had never seen before but who was evidently a classmate of my brother's. "Well, hel-lo!" he said, all sunny smiles of recognition, "aren't you Frankie's sister, Jean Kerr?" I was quite naturally outraged. "Nonsense," I said, summoning all the dignity I could muster, "she's a much younger person."

Insist That All Midnight Conferences Be Held in Somebody Else's Hotel Room

Each night after the performance it is customary for all members of the production staff to meet with the author to discuss the somber past, the doubtful future, and the plain fact that the new comedy scene which just went into the show is falling rather flatter than the old one. This session, coming as it does at the end of a perfect day, may loosen your last grip on sanity. It is nevertheless obligatory. The producer insists upon it because he is still trying to persuade you to cut that godawful scene at the end of the first act and because he is reluctant to go down to the bar and join his friends who have come up from New York to see the show. (The friends will say, "I'm gonna level with you, Lou—close it," which is why, in the theater, auld acquaintances are oft forgot and never brought to mind.) And most playwrights accept the inevitable nightly postmortem because they have learned that it is one tenth of one per cent less taxing to talk about the rewrite than to do the rewrite.

However, all of this talking should definitely be done in the producer's suite. Should the merry little band assemble in your room, not only will you have to sign the tab for all those chicken sandwiches and all that scotch, but, what is more to the point, you will have cut off your escape hatch.

Sooner or later as soft voices die and tempers rise, the

director (or maybe the producer) will see fit to add to the many true remarks spoken in jest. "Look, Sam," he will say, still smiling, "we all know the first act is lousy—what you don't seem to realize is that the *second* act stinks." At this moment you should be free to arise and go without a backward glance. It might take twenty minutes if you have to throw them all out of your room.

These nuggets of advice I am dispensing so freely are all, as you can see, concerned with protecting the sanity of the playwright. Playwrights are an unstable crew at best, and they tend to become unglued in the face of the most trivial mishaps. I remember one who was carted right back to Menninger's because, at the climactic moment of his play, the bit player who had to call for the police cried out loudly and clearly, "Help! There's been a murder—call the poloose!"

But if the author, standing at the back of the house gnashing his teeth, is painfully aware that the leading man has just answered the telephone before it rang, the audience tends to remain blissfully unconscious of technical mishaps, unless, of course, the leading lady actually tumbles off the stage into the first row of the orchestra. In this connection I recall an experience I had while tending an ailing musical in Philadelphia. For complicated reasons of the plot there was a big snowstorm effect at the finale of the show. One night the ropes that controlled the snow bags (enormous canvas bags filled with tiny pellets of white paper) somehow became intertwined with the ropes that pulled up the main curtain, so that from the beginning of the second act it snowed—gently, evenly, peacefully, down through the crystal chandeliers of the ballroom, all over the sunny farm scene, without pause during the night-club scene, it snowed on the just and unjust alike. Indeed, the prodigal flurries continued right up to the moment, at the very end of the show, when the leading lady had to say, "It's snowing, Max." She said the line looking up to the empty heavens, because by that time, naturally, we were fresh out of snow—and I sat there with my face buried in my hands, praying for guidance. When I dashed outside, still feeling murderous, I stumbled into a friend who was seeing the show for the first time. "Oh, Lord," I said, "you would have to catch this performance. Of course things go wrong every night, but this—this is the worst, the absolute worst!" He surprised me by being entirely philosophical about the whole matter. "You worry too much," he said, patting my shoulder. "Sure I noticed she was flat on that first song, but I don't think anybody else did."

By the way, many of the problems that cause faintness and loss of appetite out of town begin with simple mistakes in casting. Some performers that should never, in any circumstances, be cast are:

1 Known alcoholics. You will have trouble enough with the unknown ones.

2 Small children. It's not just that unless, happily, they are orphans, you will have to cope with their mothers. Much worse is the fact that children, being quicker, brighter, and in a better state of preservation than their elders, can and do memorize the entire script in three days.

Thereafter they conceive it to be their civic duty to prompt the star any time and every time he seems to be groping for a word. This unwise practice not only exposes the child to unsuitable language but, in general, lowers the morale and defeats the efforts of the director to create a tight ship with a happy crew.

3 Dogs. Dogs, of course, don't have mothers, which makes them a little easier to deal with, though not much. I was once connected with a production that required the services of a large English sheepdog. We began rehearsals with a beast that was supposed to be so highly trained that I imagined he would be able to do the rewrite. As it turned out, he was not trained even in the conventional sense. The circumstances over which he had no control

eventually elicited howls of outrage from the manager of the theater—in which we were rehearsing—and resulted in our being urged—in the most intemperate language imaginable—to "go hire another hall." Furthermore, this same unfortunate animal had a tendency to bite the actors during performance, which not only lost him audience sympathy but lost us several actors.

He was replaced out of town by an enchanting dog who, unlike her predecessor, was well adjusted and secure, and limited her nibbling to the bits of liver we deposited at various key points on the set. However, she commanded a salary that was well in excess of that paid to most of the company, a circumstance which did not endear her to the other performers, several of whom claimed that, in any case, she had a habit of scratching her ears on their best lines. (I don't think she did this deliberately, but then you never know; and so far as these actors were concerned, they were already unhinged from having to compete with two very cute child actors who crept into any hearts conceivably left vacant by that dog.)

In addition to talking about the pitfalls that must be sidestepped, I might say a word about the really bad moments that may be inevitable. Many playwrights have recorded their despair at being required to attend the premature closing in New York. And this is a very grim occasion for the playwright. Since objectivity doesn't begin to set in for about six months, he still doesn't grasp what happened. The play may be a poor thing, alas, but it's his own, and around the dear ruin each wish of his heart is entwined verdantly still.

To me, however, there is a worse moment. This occurs during one of the final performances out of town, after all of the changes have been made. You stand at the back of the house and observe the results of all the work, all the sleepless nights, the conferences, the rehearsals, the arguments. And the show is better, oh, definitely better, and the audience seems to be enjoying it. You should be happy—and then, suddenly, you experience a brief but exquisitely painful moment of clarity in which you realize that what you are seeing is not really the show you had in mind at all.

This always reminds me of a story about a friend of mine. One Easter she had to prepare dinner for fifteen people, counting children and relatives. For reasons of economy she decided to make a ham loaf instead of the traditional baked ham. Obviously it was going to be four times the trouble, since the recipe for the ham loaf was extremely elaborate: there were a dozen different ingredients and the whole thing had to be made in advance and allowed to "set" overnight in pineapple juice. But she went gamely ahead, convinced that she was going to produce something tastier than baked ham, if not indeed a gourmet's dish. As she took the square pink loaf out of the oven, a sinister thought crossed her mind. She cut off a little slice and tasted it, her worst suspicions confirmed. In tears she flew out of the kitchen to find her husband. "Oh, Frank," she said, "do you know what I've *got?* I've got Spam!"

All I can say is God love you, honey, if you're in Philadelphia and you've got Spam.

HOW TO COPE WITH BAD NOTICES

I don't know what doctors do in the summertime, or lawyers. But I know what writers do. They worry.

A television writer who has just completed a new pilot film worries because CBS won't give him a time slot until General Mills picks up the tab for the first thirteen weeks and General Mills won't pick up the tab until CBS gives him a time slot. A novelist worries because his new book, due in November, hasn't been sold to the book clubs, the *Reader's Digest,* or to the movies, and—if he grasps the situation correctly—that book is going to be sold from door to door by him. The playwright worries because it seems increasingly unlikely that he will get (a) a director, (b) Rosalind Russell, (c) the Morosco Theatre, (d) a third act. Actually there's a certain amount of waste worry here. He could easily telescope his problems and simply worry about whether he'll get Rosalind Russell. In that event he *will* get a director and the Morosco Theatre, and even that third act won't matter so much.

It occurs to me that since the writer is going to worry all summer anyway, he might give a moment's attention to what he will do if he gets bad notices. Now, when the problem is only theoretical, is the time to bone up on those techniques of self-preservation which, if properly applied, will save him expensive psychiatric bills later. Next Octo-

ber, when no man sleeps until the *Times* comes out, is much too late.

Let me make it clear that I am not talking about outright pans. There is really a kind of mercy about completely bad, completely disastrous notices. For one thing, they eliminate alternatives. You goofed, that's all. Even your own mother can see that you goofed. And, in the sense that one worries only while there is still hope, there is now nothing to worry about. The television series *will* disappear, the show *will* fold, the book *will* be remaindered. When the worst that *can* happen happens, it is even possible to be jaunty in the ashes. Not long ago John Osborne's new musical, *The World of Paul Slickey*, opened in London to reviews that ranged in invective from "dull and revolting" to "dull and abominable." Two days later Mr. Osborne announced, with what seemed to me astonishing aplomb, that he had received "the worst notices since Judas Iscariot."

However, it's rare that you get notices so bad you can brag about them. Most of the time the notices are "mixed," a euphemism which, in the words of George S. Kaufman, simply means that they were "good and rotten." Trouble begins for a novelist when he reads in the *Times* that his latest effort is "a tender book, a beautiful book, yes, a *great* book" and in the *Tribune* that it is "curiously disappointing." Or vice versa. The perplexed author does not always leap to the conclusion, as is so often captiously suggested, that the negative reviewer is wrong. Deep down inside he may sense a certain justice in the blast. What really hurts is his conviction that this same reviewer has been wrong all season and there seems to be no reason why he had to be correct on this particular occasion.

Nevertheless the papers are on the street, and the future must be faced. A businessman who has had reverses just goes back to the office. But a writer with a set of mixed notices can't turn around and go right back to writing. In the first place he is in shock, and even trivial things—like accidentally coming upon one page of the second carbon of the third revision under the desk blotter—cause him to break down and sob. In the second place he would have to have the persistence of a salmon and the hide of a buffalo to be unaffected by the knowledge that there is a whole body of opinion which maintains he was never able to write in the first place. (The range of the fallout can be judged when even a Dear One says, "George, do you remember how happy we used to be when you were with Equitable Life?") Since in most cases religion and family obligations preclude suicide, a writer simply has to live through the grisly six weeks during which it will become clear whether he is going to swim with the good notices or sink with the bad ones.

During this trying period, one must keep busy. A long ocean voyage, which would be ideal, is impractical since there is as yet no money to pay for it. Of course five minutes out of every day can be consumed by calling Good Old Bill in the sales department, ostensibly to inquire for his wife's bronchitis and actually to see if he has "heard anything."

But this still leaves a large part of the day unaccounted for. One might learn to speak Chinese, or perhaps do some volunteer hospital work. I am told that at a time like this a small physical impairment often proves a blessing in disguise. A television writer assured me with tears in his eyes that, but for an ailing thumb last winter, he would have "ended up in the loony bin." It seems that on the very morning he read in John Crosby's column that his new series was "a soporific, easily the equal of Nembutal," he developed a case of blood poisoning in his left thumb. (N.B. He doesn't relate this in any way to the notice.) For the next six days, on the advice of his doctor, he had to soak his hand for a whole hour, every other hour. And what with experimenting with different-size basins, trying to keep the water hot, and changing his wet shirts, he was

never able to give Crosby his full attention. Clearly this was an ideal substitute for what he really wanted to do, which was soak his head.

Confronted by an absolutely infuriating review, it is sometimes helpful for the victim to do a little personal research on the critic. Is there any truth to the rumor that he had no formal education beyond the age of eleven? In any event is he able to construct a simple English sentence? Are his modifiers misplaced? Do his participles dangle? When moved to lyricism does he write "I had a fun time"? Was he ever arrested for burglary? I don't know that you will prove anything this way, but it is perfectly harmless and quite soothing.

I myself find it therapeutic to take the very worst review and heavily underline the most offending phrases, such as "heavy-handed and lumbering" or perhaps "witless and tasteless." The next step is to paste the notice on the mirror in the bathroom, where you will be able to glance at it at odd hours. In the beginning this may cause vertigo and faintness, but in no time at all you will make the cheering discovery that the words have lost their power to maim. They have even lost their power to communicate. Recuperation is complete when the phrase "witless and tasteless" seems as quaint and meaningless as "smoking in the outer lobby only," "no U turn," or "twenty-three skiddoo," as gloriously incomprehensible as "a thinking man's filter."

If he has the heart to leave the house during this period, the writer will be forced to assume an air of hearty optimism, if only because he doesn't want to contribute to his own bad word of mouth. At the same time he must be warned that any acquaintance who says, "Sam, I didn't read the notices, how were they?" has in fact read everything, including that one-line reference in Winchell. The way to deal with this character is to mystify him. Say "Frankly, I was pretty relieved." Let *him* figure out what you're so relieved about. Or, better still, say, "Well, Bobby and Hal (the producers) are pretty happy." Just why they should be happy is unfathomable, but it sounds good, and if—later on—someone gets the reputation of being a little addled, it won't be you. Never, under any circumstances, indicate how far you had to go for a good notice by saying, "Listen, did you happen to read *The New Statesman and Leader?*"

A slightly different situation presents itself when a close friend says, "I just read that pan you got from Kerr; I don't know what he was talking about." In this instance you must fight the temptation to snap back with "Of course not—the man is an idiot." An outburst like this would not only indicate that you are a poor sport but, worse, would end the conversation then and there. The shrewd move is to adopt an air of thoughtful consideration and say, "I don't know that I agree with you, Henry—after all, Kerr is a pretty sound man and I thought many of his points were well taken." Your friend, if he is any friend at all, will be outraged at this display of sweet reason and will forthwith launch into a delightful twenty-minute tirade against Kerr.

Sometimes, in a foolish effort to get publicity and stimulate sales, a writer will agree to appear on an early-morning interview show. The idea may be appalling to him, but he has been persuaded by the press agent that, like an expensive funeral, this is the last thing he can do for the beloved. Needless to say, it's a mistake. For one thing, he will lose his sleep, which the doctor has told him is so essential right now. He will also lose sales. The interviewer, who is nothing if not plucky, will rush into the fray and show whose side she's on by stating flatly, "I loved your book, Sam—I can't think why Orville Prescott said it was stupefying." Now, alas, even those sixteen people who were as yet unacquainted with Mr. Prescott's judgment (having been mysteriously entombed in an old mine shaft on the day the review appeared) will be brought up to date.

In conclusion, it's all right to be discouraged by adverse criticism, but you don't have to be derailed. I give you the sad example of a friend of mine who read in a review of his first novel that he was "no Scott Fitzgerald," and went completely to pieces. The fact of the matter is that the poor soul never had any intention of being Scott Fitzgerald. In his secret dreams he was hot upon the Connecticut trail of Peter de Vries. Well, that's all changed now. The last time I met him he was drinking straight gin, teaching a girl columnist to read Schopenhauer, and claimed to be in the middle of a long novel called *The Gold Roller Coaster to Nowhere*.

There is, of course, one other possibility—if you are strong enough to face it. You might get all rave notices. In this event you will spend your days in suicidal gloom

brought on by the feeling that you've hit your peak and have nowhere to go but down. As a result of this destructive thinking, you will acquire an ulcer and have to give up smoking and drinking. Having given up smoking and drinking, you will get fat.

Well, it's something to worry about.

THE TEN WORST THINGS
ABOUT A MAN

Actually I feel a bit of a fraud to be picking on men when I always pretend to be so crazy about them. And, deep down inside, I am crazy about them. They are sweet, you know, and so helpful. At parties, men you've barely met will go back to the buffet to get you a muffin and they will leap to their feet to tell you that you've got the wrong end of the cigarette in your mouth. Notice that when you are trying to squeeze into a tight parking place there will always be some nice man driving by who will stick his head out the window and shout, "Lady, you've got a whole *mile* back there!"

But, charming as men are, we can't sit here and pretend they're perfect. It wouldn't be good for them, and it wouldn't be true. Marrying a man is like buying something you've been admiring for a long time in a shop window. You may love it when you get it home, but it doesn't always go with everything else in the house. One reason for this is that most men insist on behaving as though this were an orderly, sensible universe, which naturally makes them hard to live with. The other reason they're hard to live with (and I know this sounds illogical) is that they're so *good*. Perhaps I can clarify that last statement by listing a few of their more intolerable virtues.

1 A Man Will not Meddle in What He Considers His Wife's Affairs

He may interfere at the office, driving secretaries to drink and premature marriage by snooping into file drawers and tinkering with the mimeograph machine. Back home in the nest he is the very model of patience and *laissez-faire*. He will stare at you across the dining-room table (as you simultaneously carve the lamb and feed the baby) and announce, in tones so piteous as to suggest that all his dreams have become ashes, "There's no salt in this shaker."

What a wife objects to in this situation is not just the notion that Daddy has lived in this house for thirteen years without ever discovering where the salt is kept. It's more

the implication that only she has the necessary fortitude, stamina, and simple animal cunning necessary to pour the salt into that little hole in the back of the shaker.

2 A Man Remembers Important Things

It really is remarkable the fund of information he keeps at his finger tips: the date of the Battle of Hastings, the name of the man who invented the printing press, the formula for water, the Preamble to the Constitution, and every lyric Larry Hart ever wrote. It is obviously unreasonable to expect one so weighted down with relevant data to remember a simple fact like what size shirt he takes, or what grade Gilbert is in, or even that you told him fifteen times that the Bentleys were coming to dinner. A woman just has to go through life remembering for two. As an example of this, I was recently told about a wife who, from time to time, pinned a tag on her husband's overcoat. The tag read, "Please don't give me a ride home from the station. I have my own car today." However, this technique wouldn't work with my husband because he usually forgets and leaves his overcoat on the train.

3 A Man Will Try to Improve Your Mind

Working on the suspicion that women read nothing in the newspapers except bulletins from Macy's and Dorothy Kilgallen, the average man takes considerable pains to keep his scatterbrained wife *au courant* with the contemporary political situation. And we get the following dialogue:

"Did you read Walter Lippmann today on the shake-up in the Defense Department?"

"No, what did he have to say?"

"You should have read it. It was a damn good piece."

"Well, what was the gist of it?"

"Where is that paper? It should be around here someplace."

"It's not around here someplace. It went out with the garbage."

"That's too bad, because it would have clarified the whole situation for you."

"I'm sure. But what was he saying?"

"Oh, he was talking about the shake-up in the Defense Department."

"I know that, but what did he *say?*"

"He was against it."

4 A Man Allows You to Make the Important Decisions
Because he has such respect for your superior wisdom and technical know-how, he is constantly asking questions like "Does this kid need a sweater?" or "Is that baby wet?" Personally I am willing to go down through life being the court of last appeal on such crucial issues as bedtime (is it?), cookies (can they have another?), rubbers (do they have to wear them?), and baths (tonight? but they took one last night). But, just between us, I have no confidence in a man who wanders out to the kitchen, peers into the icebox, and asks plaintively, "Do I want a sandwich?"

5 A Man Will Give You an Honest Answer
If you say, "Honey, do you think this dress is too tight for me to wear?" he'll say, "Yes."

6 A Man Takes Pride in His Personal Possessions
A woman will go all her days in the wistful belief that her husband would give her the shirt off his back. Thus she is in no way prepared for the cries of outrage that will go up should she ever be rash enough to take the shirt off his back. It doesn't matter that the shirt in question has a torn pocket, a frayed collar, and has, in any case, been at the bottom of the clothes hamper for three years. It's his, and you wear it at your risk.

My husband will say to me, "What are you doing in that shirt, for heaven's sake?" Now he doesn't really want to know what I'm doing. He can see what I'm doing. I'm painting the garage doors. He just wants me to know that

124

that shirt was near and dear to him, and now, as a result of my vandalism, it's totally ruined.

There are two possible solutions to this problem. You can hire a painter to paint the garage doors, or you can dye the shirt purple so he won't be able to recognize it.

7 A Man Believes in Sharing

Men are all advocates of togetherness, up to a point. They will agree that it is "our house," "our mortgage," and, of course, "our song." It is interesting, however, to observe the circumstances under which items that once were "our" joint concern suddenly become your exclusive possession. For instance, a man will return from a stroll through "our back yard" to tell you, "Honey, I think your daffodils are getting clump-bound." Or, on another occasion, "I see that the hinge is off your medicine chest." In my opinion, this policy of dissociating from anything that is temporarily out of order reaches its ultimate confusion with statements like "Hey, your man is here to fix the chimney." My man? I never saw him before in my life.

8 A Man Doesn't Want You to Worry

Since he supposes, and quite correctly, that you worry a great deal about his health, he will go to any lengths to spare you the least alarm about his physical condition. He will say, as though it were the most casual thing in the world, "Well, I almost keeled over in Grand Central today."

"Good Lord," you will say, "what happened?"

"Nothing, nothing. I leaned against a pillar and I didn't actually fall down."

"But honey, what happened? Did you feel faint? You didn't have a terribly sharp pain in your chest, did you?"

"Oh, no. No, nothing like that."

"Well, what do you mean you almost keeled over?"

"I almost keeled over, that's all."

"But there must have been some *reason.*"

"Oh, I guess it's that foot again."

"What foot again? Which foot?"

"Oh, I told you about my foot."

"You most certainly did not tell me anything about your foot."

"The one that's been numb since last summer."

"*Your foot has been numb since last summer?*"

"Now it's more like the whole leg."

"Good heavens, let's call the doctor. Let's call this minute!"

"Why?"

"Why? Are you out of your mind? Because there's something the matter with your leg, that's why!"

"See, there you go, flying off again. I'm sorry I mentioned it, and there's nothing the matter with my leg, nothing."

9 *A Man Is Reasonable*

Actually there is nothing wrong with a man's being reasonable so long as he doesn't insist on your being reasonable along with him. "Let's be *reasonable*," he keeps say-

ing with about the same frequency that he says, "Go ask your mother," and "What's for dinner?" The occasions on which he thinks you should be reasonable vary, but on the whole it's safe to say that it's any time you're driven past your endurance and out of your mind by shiftless department stores (who promised faithfully to deliver that crib three weeks ago) and irresponsible cleaning women (who simply don't show up on the day you're having sixteen people to dinner). At times like these, a woman wishes only a word of sympathy, like "Yes, yes, they're all a bad lot." And any man who urges his wife to be reasonable and to consider the possibility that Hattie may really *have* "the virus" deserves to wax all the floors himself.

10 A Man Idealizes His Wife

This is another way of saying that he hasn't really looked at her in fourteen years. To get me a housecoat for my birthday, my husband will make the unthinkable sacrifice of entering Lord & Taylor's and even penetrating the awesome portals of the lingerie department. There, as I reconstruct the scene later, he selects the slimmest, trimmest little salesgirl on the floor and announces, "She's about your size." Naturally I have to take the thing back and get one four sizes larger.

On second thought, I shouldn't complain about that. If you stop and think, it's really rather charming of him.

128

HAPPY MOTORING

We still have the first car we ever bought, shortly after the abdication of Edward VII. And, since it still goes front-ward and backward, we weren't even thinking of buying a new one. Actually, we felt that our car had aged like a fine old wine. Perhaps it does tremble all over when the wheels hit a seam in the pavement, but no more than a high-spirited horse. And talk about *faithful!* Why, I could tell you stories about that little car. . . .

But why do I torment myself, now that everything has changed? Last week we went to the movies and left the car in a parking lot. I gave the man thirty-five cents and was waiting for a stub when he said quietly, "Lady, you don't need a ticket—I can remember this one." At first I thought he was referring to the sand pails and the bathing suits which could be seen through the snow on the back window ledge. But it came to me later (a great many things came to me later on account of the movie, which was about this teen-ager who was misunderstood by everybody, especially me) that our venerable, trusty sedan was a source of merriment to the entire staff of Maple Street Parking. That young man was implying—implying nothing, he as much as said—that it was an antique, an eyesore, and a menace to the orderly progress of traffic on the Post Road. Isn't it strange that so often an outsider will be the first to notice that a loved one is failing?

So, we're in the market for a new car. We've looked at some and they certainly are beautiful—longer, lower, faster, richer, milder. But where, I ask you, are those little features one looks for in a family car? I know they've been working day and night in Detroit achieving such wonders as power steering, which will enable you to get out of a tight parking place without so much as bending your elbows—in the unlikely event that you are able to find a tight parking place. I've heard about push-button driving and air conditioning and I say hail, Henry Ford, cheers, General Motors, but what I want is a towel rack in the back seat. And if the children are going to insist on *chocolate* frozen custard it might be safer to have two towel racks.

Also, I'd like to have galvanized fencing installed from

floor to ceiling just behind the front seat. This might just possibly keep small children in the back seat, and, what is more to the point, it should discourage their efforts to drop all the change from their lunch money down the back of your neck while you're driving.

I'm dreaming wildly now, but wouldn't it be nice for families with more than two children to have a car without any windows at all in the back? Not only would this eliminate all arguments about whose turn it is to sit next to the window, it would keep the children who are old enough to read from constantly informing you that you are now six mi., four mi., and one mi. away from a restaurant that features more than twenty different flavors of ice cream. Of course without back windows you wouldn't have a rear view, but do you anyway—with the ice skates, cowboy hats, and one pair of skis piled in the back?

By the way, do you know that it is possible to get a twenty-six-inch bicycle into the back seat of an average car? What isn't possible is to get it out. What also isn't possible is to find a parking place in front of the bicycle-repair shop, so that you have to double-park in the roaring traffic's boom while you try frantically to claw the bike free now that the handlebars are entangled with the door handle. I find that the simplest and most efficient thing to do is just to lay your head on the hood of the car and moan. Sooner or later you will attract a crowd and it won't be too difficult for three men, working as a team, to get that bike out of there. Of course, they will tear the upholstery, but then it's never been the same since the baby was carsick.

What would be a help is not, heaven forbid, a larger back-seat area (then we'd be carting sailboats up to have them varnished) but two large hooks on the roof of the car from which you could hang the bicycle. Or a teeter-totter, to mention another item that I know positively will not fit inside a car.

Nobody else seems to have this next problem, so what I am going to suggest might not prove a popular feature. But, speaking for myself, I'd like the floor of the car lined with nails so nobody could stretch out down there. I find that I can drive through heavy traffic with one boy lying on the floor in his good clothes drinking a Coke. What unhinges me completely and leads to so many insults from passing male drivers is when three of them try to lie on the floor, shouting, "We've got our eyes shut, say when we're passing the post office! Are we near Futterman's? Did we turn onto Beach?" Someday one of them is going

to open his eyes and ask, "And why did you drive into this deep water, Mommy?" And Mommy will tell them.

But these are all trifles, the icing on the cake. What I really want, and what would contribute most to the joyous sense of family togetherness on those Sunday trips to Playland, would be a little bathroom in the back seat. Don't ask me how, I'm not an engineer. This is something that will have to be worked out at the factory.

MY WILD IRISH MOTHER

I'm never going to write my autobiography and it's all my mother's fault. I didn't hate her, so I have practically no material. In fact, the situation is worse than I'm pretending. We were crazy about her—and you know I'll never get a book out of that, much less a musical.

Mother was born Kitty O'Neill, in Kinsale, Ireland, with bright red hair, bright blue eyes, and the firm conviction that it was wrong to wait for an elevator if you were only going up to the fifth floor. It's not just that she won't wait for elevators, which she really feels are provided only for the convenience of the aged and infirm. I have known her to reproach herself on missing one section of a revolving door. And I well remember a time when we missed a train from New York to Washington. I fully expected her to pick up our suitcases and announce, "Well, darling, the exercise will be good for us."

When I have occasion to mutter about the financial problems involved in maintaining five children in a large house, Mother is quick to get to the root of the problem. "Remember," she says, "you take cabs a lot." In Mother's opinion, an able-bodied woman is perfectly justified in taking a taxi to the hospital if her labor pains are closer than ten minutes apart.

The youngest daughter of wealthy and indulgent parents, Mother went to finishing schools in France and to the Royal Conservatory of Music in London. Thus, when she came to America to marry my father, her only qualifications for the role of housewife and mother were the ability to speak four languages, play three musical instruments, and make blancmange. I, naturally, wasn't around during those first troubled months when Mother learned to cook. But my father can still recall the day she boiled corn on the cob, a delicacy unknown in Ireland at that time, for five hours until the cobs were tender. And, with a typical beginner's zeal, Mother "put up" twenty bushels of tomatoes that first winter, before it struck her that neither she nor Dad really liked canned tomatoes.

By the time I was old enough to notice things, Mother was not only an excellent cook. She could make beer, an accomplishment that set her apart and endeared her to many in those Prohibition days. Of course, Mother didn't drink beer, so it was hard for her to judge whether she was on the right track or not. And it was always an anxious moment when my father took his first sip of each new batch and declared, "Yes, Kit, I think you're getting warmer."

But beer brewing is a very involved process, as the Budweiser people will tell you, and the crock used to stand for weeks in the pantry before it was time for the bottling. I don't know how big the crock was, but I know that it stood taller than I did. One of my earliest memories—I must have been four—is of sitting on the floor handing the bottle caps to Mother. On this particular occasion the crock was nearly empty when Mother gave a little shriek. Something, something—perhaps a mouse—was at the bottom of the crock.

She took a long fork and gingerly fished out a small, sodden object. I knew in a flash what it was, but I was too terrified to speak. Then I heard Mother say, in a very strained voice, "Jean, you must *always* tell Mommy where you put your shoes."

Together we sat in silence and stared at the rows and rows of shiny bottles all ready to go into the cases down in the cellar. Then Mother jumped up. A thought had struck her. She tossed the shoe into the garbage and announced briskly, "You know what? I think it will help the aging process." And it must have, too, because everyone said it was the best batch she ever made.

Just as she made beer she never drank, Mother would cook things she had no intention of eating. Where food is concerned, she is totally conservative. She will study the menu at an expensive restaurant with evident interest and then say, "Darling, where do you see lamb chops?" Or she will glance with real admiration at a man at a nearby table who seems actually to be consuming an order of cherrystone clams. "Aren't Americans marvelous?" she'll remark, "They will eat anything."

On the other hand she was always willing to prepare all manner of exotic dishes for Dad and the rest of us. In the old days the men who worked for my father frequently gave him gifts of game—venison, rabbit, and the like. Occasionally we children would protest. I recall becoming quite tearful over the prospect of eating deer, on the theory that it might be Bambi. But Mother was always firm. "Nonsense," she would say. "Eat up, it's just like chicken."

But one night she went too far. I don't know where she got this enormous slab of meat; I don't think my father brought it home. It stood overnight in the icebox in some complicated solution of brine and herbs. The next day the four of us were told that we could each invite a friend to dinner. Mother spent most of the day lovingly preparing her roast. That night there were ten of us around the dining-room table, and if Mother seemed too busy serving all the rest of us to eat anything herself, that was not at all unusual. At this late date I have no impression of what the meat tasted like. But I know that we were all munching away when Mother beamed happily at us and asked, "Well, children, how are you enjoying the bear?"

Forks dropped and certain of the invited guests made emergency trips to the bathroom. For once, all of Mother's protestations that it was just like chicken were unavailing. Nobody would touch another bite. She was really dismayed. I heard her tell Dad, "It's really strange, Tom—I thought all Americans liked bear."

Mother's education, as I have indicated, was rather one-sided. While she knew a great deal about such "useless" things as music and art and literature, she knew nothing whatever, we were quick to discover, about isosceles triangles or watts and volts or the Smoot-Hawley Tariff. As we were growing up, we made haste to repair these gaps.

One of the most charming things about Mother was the extraordinary patience with which she would allow us youngsters to "instruct" her. I remember my brother Hugh, when he was about eight, sitting on the foot of Mother's

bed and giving her a half-hour lecture which began with the portentous question, "Mom, how much do you know about the habits of the common housefly?"

At that, it's remarkable how much of this unrelated information stayed with her. Just recently I was driving her to a train and she noticed, high up in the air, a squirrel that was poised on a wire that ran between two five-story buildings. "Look at that little squirrel 'way up on that wire," she said. "You know, if he gets one foot on the ground, he'll be electrocuted."

But if her knowledge of positive and negative electricity is a little sketchy, there is nothing sketchy about her knowledge of any subject in which she develops an interest. Mother always adored the theater and was a passionate playgoer from the time she was five years old. However, during the years when she was sobbing gently over *The Lily of Killarney* in Cork City, she was blissfully unaware of the menacing existence of American drama critics or the fact that their printed opinions had a certain measurable effect on the box office. Even when she came to America, she still had the feeling that five nights was probably an impressive run for a Broadway show.

Time passed, and my husband and I became involved in the theater. Mother began to get the facts. When, about ten years ago, we were living in Washington and came up to New York for the opening of a revue we had written, I promised Mother that I would send her all the reviews, special delivery, as soon as they appeared. In those days, before the demise of *The Sun*, there were eight metropoli-

tan dailies. Eventually we got hold of all the papers and I
was able to assess the evidence. All but one of the morning
papers were fine, and while there were certain quibbles
in the afternoon papers, the only seriously negative notice
appeared in *The Sun*. Ward Morehouse was then the
critic on *The Sun* but happened to be out of town at the
moment, and the review was written by his assistant, or,
as I was willing to suppose, his office boy. So, with that
special brand of feminine logic that has already made my
husband prematurely gray, I decided to omit this particular notice in the batch I was sending to my mother,
on the theory that (a) it wasn't written by the *real* critic,
and (b) nobody in Scranton, Pennsylvania, knew there
was a paper called *The Sun* anyway. This was a serious
miscalculation on my part, as I realized later in the day
when I got Mother's two-word telegram. It read, "Where's
Morehouse?"

Let me say that her interest in the more technical as-

pects of the theater continues unabated. Not long ago we were in Philadelphia, deep in the unrefined bedlam that surrounds any musical in its tryout stage. The phone rang. It was Mother. Without any preliminary word of greeting, she asked in hushed, conspiratorial tones, "Darling, have you pointed and sharpened?"

"Good Lord, Mother," I said, "what are you talking about?"

"I'm talking about the show, dear," she said, sounding like a small investor, which she was. "*Variety* says it needs pointing and sharpening, and I think we should listen to them."

To the four low-metabolism types she inexplicably produced, Mother's energy has always seemed awesome. "What do you think," she's prone to say, "do I have time to cut the grass before I stuff the turkey?" But her whirlwind activity is potentially less dangerous than her occasional moments of repose. Then she sits, staring into space, clearly lost in languorous memories. The faint, fugitive smile that hovers about her lips suggests the gentle melancholy of one hearing Mozart played beautifully. Suddenly she leaps to her feet. "I know it will work," she says. "All we have to do is remove that wall, plug up the windows, and extend the porch."

It's undoubtedly fortunate that she has the thrust and the energy of a well-guided missile. Otherwise she wouldn't get a lick of work done, because everybody who comes to her house, whether to read the gas meter or to collect for UNICEF, always stays at least an hour. I used to think that they were one and all beguiled by her Irish accent. But I have gradually gleaned that they are telling her the story of their invariably unhappy lives. "Do you remember my lovely huckleberry man?" Mother will ask. "Oh, *yes*, you do—he had red hair and ears. Well, his brother-in-law sprained his back and hasn't worked in six months, and we're going to have to take a bundle of clothes over to those children." Or again, "Do you remember that nice girl in the Scranton Dry Goods? Oh, yes you do, she was in lamp shades and she had gray hair and wore gray dresses. Well, she's having an operation next month and you must remember to pray for her." Mother's credo, by the way, is that if you want something, anything, don't just sit there—pray for it. And she combines a Job-like patience in the face of the mysterious ways of the Almighty with a flash of Irish rebellion which will bring her to say—and I'm sure she speaks for many of us—"Jean, what I am really looking for is a blessing that's *not* in disguise."

She does have a knack for penetrating disguises, whether it be small boys who claim that they have taken baths or middle-aged daughters who swear that they have lost five pounds. She has a way of cutting things to size, particularly books, which she gobbles up in the indiscriminate way that a slot machine gobbles up quarters. I sent her a novel recently because it had a Welsh background and because the blurb on the jacket declared, "Here is an emotional earthquake—the power and glory of a great love story combined with the magic of childhood." Later, I asked her if she liked it. "Not really," she said. "It was nothing but fornication, all seen through the eyes of a nine-year-old boy." Some time ago I had a collection of short pieces brought out in book form and I sent one of the first copies to Mother. She was naturally delighted. Her enthusiasm fairly bubbled off the pages of the letter. "Darling," she wrote, "isn't it marvelous the way those old pieces of yours finally came to the surface like a dead body!"

I knew when I started this that all I could do was list the things Mother says, because it's not possible, really, to describe her. All my life I have heard people break off their lyrical descriptions of Kitty and announce helplessly, "You'll just have to meet her."

However, I recognize, if I cannot describe, the lovely festive air she always brings with her, so that she can arrive any old day in July and suddenly it seems to be Christmas Eve and the children seem handsomer and better behaved and all the adults seem more charming and—

Well, you'll just have to meet her.

WHEN I WAS QUEEN OF THE MAY

Our eight-year-old Johnny was looking for a bottle of cherry soda the other day and, after a brief, despairing survey of the bottles in the refrigerator, he slammed the door shut and asked me, quite seriously, "Mom, were you ever Miss Rheingold?"

I tried to explain to him that consumption of the product, however enthusiastic, was not the real basis for this singular honor. Eventually he grasped the picture, but I could see that it reopened avenues of uncomfortable speculation. Just last winter he had discovered that I couldn't do long division or make divinity fudge. And now this. In a wan effort to regain my lost glamour I told him about the time I was Queen of the May.

I was, at that time, a tall, gangly, giggly thirteen, and a freshman in a seminary for girls. The first hint of the celebrity that was to be mine came when I read on the bulletin board that I must report to the principal's office. I was struck numb with terror, because the only other time I had been thus summoned was after it became known that I was the girl who dared Bunny Ryan to peek over the heavy curtain that separated Sister Mary Olive's bed from all the other beds in the dormitory. (Bunny reported that she had hair all right, but it was very short.) But to-day I could sense, as soon as I stepped into the office, that I wasn't in serious trouble. For one thing, Mother Claire didn't fix on her pince-nez, a thing she always did when displeased. I don't know whether she thought it made her look more severe, or whether she simply wanted to get a better look at the offender.

Mother Claire was a saintly old lady of great sweetness and strange sibilance due, I now suppose, to ill-fitting false teeth. She never spoke above a whisper and one could follow her progress down the narrow corridors by the gentle tapping of a cane and a trail of hissing s's. Her standard method of greeting, wherever she encountered us and whatever the occasion, was to raise a powdery white hand and whisper, "S-s-s-softly, young ladies, s-s-softly." Mother was so far from being self-conscious about this impediment that it seemed almost as if she chose her phrases for the difficulties they presented. "Stick-to-it-iveness is necessary for success" she said umpteen times a day, regally unaware of the small storm of whistling consonants that broke about our ears. But such was her air of gentle authority that not one of us would have dreamed of smiling. Nor did we ever mimic her at recess the way we did Sister Stanislaus, who used to clear her throat three times before she spoke and then say, in hushed, melancholy tones, "A girl who would chew gum will smoke, and a girl who would smoke will drink, and a girl who would drink [pregnant pause]—well, I think you know what that kind of a girl will do." We did, too, or thought we did, and we shuddered deliciously at the fearful prospect.

But Mother was a little island quite removed from our girlish jocularity. On that afternoon, when she said to me, "My dear, I see that you are growing in nature and in grace," I blushed with pleasure quite as if I didn't know that, at one time or another, she had said the same thing to every girl in the school. "Thank you, Mother," I said, curtsying so low that, to my horror, an old yellow comb in a rather forlorn condition fell out of my uniform pocket and clattered to the floor. Mother ignored the comb and my furtive efforts to reclaim it and said, "You will be gratified to learn that your good teachers have chosen you to crown the statue of Our Lady in the grove." I was more than gratified, I was stunned.

In the ordinary course of things there would have been nothing noteworthy about a crowning. Every year on the first of May each class had a private ceremony in which the statues of Our Lady (and there were sometimes two or three in a single classroom) were banked with flowers and crowned with wreaths. Indeed, such was our reputation for zeal in this matter that the girls in a neighboring public school spread the entirely false rumor that we seminarians, in our anxiety to lay laurel on every available plaster head, had inadvertently crowned the bust of Chopin in the music room.

What made this year's crowning a special event was the fact that, for the first time, we were going to crown the massive stone statue that stood in the grove midway between the school and the old folks' home. The statue had been there from time immemorial. (Bunny Ryan said her grandmother remembered it from the time she was a little girl, and since her grandmother had once written to Abraham Lincoln one sensed that we were in direct contact with antiquity.) What was new, brand new, was the concrete path that wound its way through the rocks and brambles which had hitherto made formal processions out of the question and limited visitors to the shrine to those solitary pilgrims who used to dash out to the grove for an eleventh-hour "Hail Mary" just before a Latin exam.

Now, with the way paved in concrete, all things were possible, and Mother Claire had decreed that this May there would be a formal procession of the entire school, including even the babies in kindergarten who only came half day. All of us were to wear white—pure, stainless white —right down to our toes, and that meant white cotton stockings. This last was a great blow to the seniors (who were by this time wearing silk stockings) and great clusters of them sat on the window sills before class and muttered darkly about certain persons who were "positively *prehistoric*, forcryingoutloud."

Anyway, we knew the great day was nigh and we had all been supposing that Denise Macy would be chosen to do the crowning. She had two aunts in the convent, and it was known that she had obtained a doctor's certificate excusing her from gym only because it was such an affront to her modesty to appear publicly in those blue serge bloomers. Furthermore, and this was very much to the point, her uncle had donated the eleven hundred dollars for the paving of the path.

But Denise had been passed over and I had been chosen. Why? I simply couldn't understand it. If the selection had been made on the basis of brains, why not Rosemary Schuette, who was so smart that she used to correct the pronunciation of the French teacher and, according to her roommate, frequently wrote torrid love letters to her boy friend in Latin? Alas, I would never have been chosen for my beauty, even though I had been secretly using Stillman's Freckle Cream for two months and felt that my complexion, though temporarily scaly, was much improved. Actually I had a rather realistic view of my physical charms because, as a small child, I had once overheard my mother announce to a friend on the telephone, "Jean's a plain little thing, but we think she's going to be intelligent."

No, it couldn't be brains and it wouldn't be beauty, so

what was it, then—goodness? I honestly didn't feel that I was very good, but, falling into the trap of even saints and mystics, I decided that the very fact that I didn't think I was good meant that I was humble. Taking logic a step farther, it had to be granted that a humble person was a good person. It seemed clear enough when you put it that way.

I went home and told my family, but their enthusiasm was a little dampened by the fact that this honor involved the purchase of a white dress. To tell the truth, my mother was still feeling put out because she had had to pay a dress-maker four dollars to make me a sateen Herod costume last Christmas when my entire part consisted in saying fiercely, "Find the Babe, find Him and *kill* Him!"

The day we went dress hunting my mother swished her way through a whole rack of rather mournful-looking crepe-silk dresses before she called out to the salesgirl,

"Surely you have something in size sixteen besides these burial robes?" Eventually the salesgirl produced a white organdy sprinkled all over with red dots. Mother dismissed my anguished cries that it had to be *white*, all white, by saying reasonably, "In the name of God, girl, you want to get another *turn* out of it, don't you?" Quite apart from the red dots, the dress had a little capelet instead of the long sleeves that had been officially prescribed. But my protests were unavailing. Mother's mind was made up—clearly this investment was not going to be the total loss she had supposed—and she said to the salesgirl, "Wrap it up," and to me, "This won't be the first pair of elbows they've seen up there."

On the morning of the great day I crept quaking into the auditorium full of girls in their pristine white dresses,

looking and feeling like a bad case of measles. In my heart
I fully expected that I would be replaced as crowner. However, when Mother Claire finally caught sight of me and
my dots, she merely shut her eyes. A brief look of pain
washed over her face. It was the expression you might expect if the chef at Pavillon were asked to contemplate a
frozen TV dinner. But she said nothing, and clearly I was
to crown as planned.

We assembled out in the driveway, where the nun who
taught gym and was thought to have a feeling for organi-
zation pulled and pushed us into an orderly file. I was first,
accompanied by a tiny girl from the kindergarten who car-
ried the wreath on a silver tray. Then there were four music
students with flutes, who were to provide the accompani-
ment for the hymns. Next came six first-grade girls with
baskets of flowers. These were followed by the rest of the
school, paired off in twos according to height. There was a
slight feeling of uneasiness in the ranks because, owing to
the rain yesterday, the dress rehearsal had been held in
the gym and now, with the vast difference in terrain, we
felt all turned around. Still, there were no mishaps as the
procession wound its slow, solemn way to the shrine.

On arrival, the wreath bearer and I stepped forward
while all the other girls fanned out until they had formed
three large circles around the shrine. Then, after a warning
tweet from the flutes, we sang "'Tis May." I was beginning
to feel nervous: the crowning hymn came next.

"'Tis May" proved to be very effective because the five
girls who always flatted on the final high C did remember

to drop out before the end, as instructed. At last the crowning hymn began. I listened very carefully, for there was a definite place in the lyric indicating the moment when the crowner was to step forward.

It came. The voices rang out high and sweet in the open air, "Oh, Gray-shus Queen of Hea-von, we haste to-oo crown thee-ee now." Then a silence fell—the song was to be continued after the actual crowning—as I picked up the wreath and walked slowly up to the statue.

It was then that I realized, and with a stab to the heart, why I had been chosen. I had been chosen because I was the tallest girl in the school. It was equally clear, as I peered at the massive stone figure looming four or five feet above me, that, tall as I was, I wasn't tall enough. Hoping for further instructions, I shot a look of desperation and panic over to the right, where the nuns were standing in a little clump. But their heads were bowed in benediction and they seemed totally unaware of the crisis.

Finally Alice McClain, who was class president and a girl of some resourcefulness, signaled the flutes to start up again. Once more the voices sang out, though not, of course, with the same dash: "Oh, Gray-shus Queen of Hea-von, we haste to-oo crown thee-ee now." This time the word "now" seemed a reproach. Was it possible, I wondered, that we would all have to stand here until I grew another six inches?

Just as it seemed fearfully likely that the singing was going to begin for a third time, I remembered Mother Claire's oft-repeated adage, "Desperate diseases require

154

desperate remedies." I took the wreath firmly in my two hands, grasping it like a basketball, and hurled it up onto the head of the statue. For a brief moment it looked as though I had succeeded, for the wreath seemed to be resting firmly on the prongs of the stone crown. But then, slowly and majestically, it slid down until it settled rakishly over one large stone eye. The effect was decidedly disreputable, and there was a hiss of horror from the nuns as well as a gasp from the girls that quickly degenerated into muffled laughter. The first to be affected were the flautists, who, in an effort to suppress their giggles, had blown spit into their flutes and rendered them useless. The singers, without a flute to guide them, fell silent. The little girl who had borne the wreath burst into tears, and a first-grade flower girl was heard to inquire loudly, "Is it over?"

This was all too much for Mother Claire, who wheeled slowly in her tracks and marched back to the school, followed by the other nuns. Only the gym teacher remained to see that the retreat didn't turn into a rout.

I stood there, bleary with grief, feeling like the captain of a ship that was going down with all aboard. In my own mind I was the innocent victim of fate, but I knew perfectly well that in the minds of the departing nuns I was now an irresponsible defiler of sacred objects. Suddenly I broke out of line and ran down the path until I caught up with Mother Claire. "Oh, Mother," I said, the tears splattering down my cheeks, "I am sorry." Mother put on her pince-nez and looked at me. "Dots," she said sadly, "and now this." "But Mother—" I explained in what may be

the most poignant statement ever made by a thirteen-year-old, "I'm *only* five feet nine."

Even great disasters have a way of being forgotten (who today talks about the Chicago fire?) and pretty soon everybody stopped discussing the crowning and my unworthy part in it. Nevertheless it was instrumental in changing my life, because two days later I was invited to join the Seven-Uppers. This was a club formed by the seven most popular girls in the school, girls of such incomparable chic and elegance that I had aspired to be one of them only in the dim, helpless way that a copy boy aspires to be managing editor. They had evidently decided that my errors on crowning day were all part of a calculated plan and that, however roughhewn my appearance, I was to be regarded as a cutup and a card. Under these decidedly false pretenses, I joined the Seven-Uppers (there was some talk of changing the name to the Eight-Teens, but that died out). Now I, too, rode in raffish splendor in Dottie Long's maroon roadster after school. And with the others I huddled under the porch at recess and puffed away at an Old Gold. I had come a long way.

MIRROR, MIRROR, ON THE WALL, I DON'T WANT TO HEAR ONE WORD OUT OF YOU

I'm tired of all this nonsense about beauty being only skin-deep. That's deep enough. What do you want—an adorable pancreas? Personally, I find that it's work, work, work just trying to keep this top half inch in shape.

And while I'm on the subject, the first rumor I want to scotch is that I don't *care* how I look. Care? Why, I haven't even read *The Leopard,* I've been so busy reading every single one of those articles which insist that I can be a younger, lovelier me this summer. Actually I intended to be a lovelier, younger me last winter, but what with one thing and another (we had to put in new formica around the kitchen sink, and the oil burner broke down) I never got around to it. But from now on there will be no more excuses. I am going to mend my fences and learn the trick of artful make-up.

I think I ought to make it clear that I am not primarily concerned with my social appearance. If I turn up at dinner parties with that tousled, straight-from-the-haystack look that is so unaccountably attractive in Italian movie actresses I don't think it matters, because I happen to have this little trick which always endears me to hostesses. I invariably ask the young children who pass the stuffed celery what grade they are in. In fact I keep the conversational ball aloft a moment longer by musing reflectively, "Fifth grade—just imagine that." Of course one does have to look right at the children or, at the very least, keep in mind that they push on and age just like the rest of us. Imagine my surprise last week when I asked a young man who was urging a sixth deviled egg upon me, "and what grade are you in, dear?"—only to learn that he was in Harvard Law.

Nevertheless I feel I am rather sweet at dinner parties; let other women be chic and gorgeous. The one place I have simply got to look better is Bloomingdale's, when I go in there to buy face powder. It has been my practice in the past to double-park the car and dash into the store with

the air of one arriving at Radio City Music Hall two minutes before the prices change. (I always leave the motor running so the policeman can feel pretty sure I'm going to be right back.)

Now it's a curious fact that I can go into Housewares and stand among the pots for thirty-five minutes without attracting the attention of a single salesgirl, all of whom appear to be working out logarithms on their little pads. But in Cosmetics I get attention, immediate attention. The salesgirls as far away as Perfume drop everything and gather about me, making little clucking sounds. They really respond with the amiable ferocity and instinctive good will of a bevy of well-trained St. Bernards coming upon a stiffened form in an Alpine pass. At last—here is someone they can *help*.

May they suggest a blossom-pink make-up base? Do I need a herbal facial mask? What about a rich skin food for those fine lines? It is fruitless in these circumstances to explain that I already have enough cosmetics in my bathroom to make up every single extra in *The Ten Commandments*. They see what they see. And what they see is a pale-beige face that blends, in a way that is almost uncanny, with the raincoat I'm wearing, which happens to belong to my husband. Before I left the house I did apply a quick smudge of that purple lipstick somebody left in the guest room two years ago, but there is only my word for that. Right now, as I can plainly see for myself in the large mirror on the counter, I look exactly like a peeled grape—a condition which is not really appetizing even in a grape.

Of *course* I need a herbal facial mask and a cream to give new life and luxuriance to my eyelashes and a lotion to remove those telltale signs of age. And it's nice that I'm going to have something for those signs of age, because I have definitely aged in the last five minutes, and those fine lines are now becoming furrows as I realize—with mounting panic—that I have just spent twenty-eight dollars on assorted cosmetics when what I really need is a box of face powder and a raincoat of my own.

As I tear myself away from these ministering maidens (I know they think I am returning to my coal barge) I keep wishing I could somehow convey to them that, all appearances to the contrary, I do have a conscience—style and beauty-wise. If they but knew that before the discovery of the hydrogen bomb I used to spend *all* my time worrying about my dry skin. Anyway, the next time I go into that store I will be wearing three layers of make-up, all exquisitely applied. And the salesgirl will no more think of urging an extra product on me than an art-supply dealer would dream of pressing Picasso into trying a new burnt umber.

Left to my own devices, I will buy only sensible, useful cosmetics. Unlike some women, I can tell whether a cream is an absolute necessity merely by reading the advertising. I can also tell whether it's intended for me. For instance, if the ad begins: "*At last*—an entirely new concept of skin care intended for you who are tired of trying every new skin cream that comes on the market," it has to mean me because I *am* tired of trying every new skin cream that comes on the market.

Now, fully alerted, I read on to discover that "After four years of careful laboratory experimentation, Mildred Rosnick announces 'Formula 22,' a cream made exclusively from the lungs of young goldfish."

There, don't you just know that will help? I mean, you have only to pause and consider how clear-eyed and spruce even a middle-aged goldfish looks to realize that Mildred Rosnick has stumbled onto something pretty important. And I will have to act fast, because they make it pretty clear that their special introductory offer of a one-ounce jar @ $12.98 will be good for a limited time only. While $12.98 does seem a little high, I want no one to tell me that Mildred Rosnick can whip up her Formula 22 for a mere nine cents a jar. Listen, she has that whole laboratory full of technicians and goldfish and you don't feed them on peanuts.

Speaking of wet-blanket attitudes, my husband has a different angle altogether. He is always trying to explain to me that dermatologists have proven that lard, or even bacon drippings, will do just as much or just as little to lubricate the human skin as any cosmetic ever invented. Now I ask you, if dermatologists had really proven anything as ridiculous as that, wouldn't we all know about it? And another thing. When I consider the dreadful samples of lumbering humor I am subjected to when I apply the merest dab of Formula 22 ("Oh, you're coming to bed?

With all that grease, I thought you were getting ready to swim the Channel") I can't bring myself even to contemplate the low-comedy scenes we'd have if I came to bed covered with bacon fat.

Of course the thing about my husband is that he is not really on this planet. He's the kind of man who will come home from a cocktail party and tell you about the fascinating conversation he had with a new editor at Simon and Schuster who feels that all these new beat-generation authors are merely a reflection of the mass protest against the thermonuclear potential. I mean, that's his idea of a gossipy tidbit. Later, I will hear that *she* was one of the guests, and I will fly at him accusingly. "Listen, Peggy says that Marilyn Monroe was at that party." And he will say, "That's right, I guess she was." And a man like that will presume to give advice.

I'm sure it would be a help in any program of beauty to set oneself a simple goal. Personally, I concentrate on

keeping myself in a state of repair just sufficient to stop people asking me if I remember how charming Ethel Barrymore was on the opening night of *Captain Jinks of the Horse Marines.*

But one can set one's sights too high. Just last week in the beauty parlor I witnessed a poignant example of this very thing. A rather mousy matron handed the hairdresser a picture of Suzy Parker, her lovely Edwardian profile glimmering beneath a mass of tossed-salad curls. "See," the lady explained rather ingenuously, "this is the way I want to look." Honey, we all do. But a mountaineer doesn't *start* with Everest.

I try to pick a model closer at hand, like any one of those young women who appear on the society pages handing each other checks for the Milk Fund. What an elegant crew they are—so svelte in black, so chaste in that solitary strand of pearls. "Lovely Mrs. Philip van Rensselaer Skylark III," I read, quite consumed with envy, "is celebrated for her candlelight suppers. Though Mrs. Skylark is the proud possessor of two young daughters, three whippets, and a myna bird, she still finds time to help the North Shore Hospital." Well, that's the way I'm going to look even if it means that I have to help the North Shore Hospital.

Looking back over these paragraphs, I sense the absence of that one piece of constructive advice that might save this from being simply another self-reproaching sermon entitled "Once I Was Considered Plain—Today I Am a Mess." Luckily I have just remembered not one, but two definite rituals for beauty that have been *known to work*.

1 *How to Be Adorable, though Pregnant* Actually this is much simpler than it seems. The mother-to-be should get her hair set, apply a rosy-pink make-up, put on her most becoming maternity frock, and—here we get to the important part—climb into bed and pull the covers up under her arms. In this position she will feel chic. Overheated, perhaps, but chic.

As a matter of fact I have never been able to follow

this prescription to the letter because I wear a size eighteen, and, as you may know, it is practically impossible to buy a maternity dress, becoming or otherwise, in size eighteen. The manufacturers seem to operate on the unquestionably sound premise that a woman who takes a size eighteen is already in sufficient trouble and has no business getting pregnant. Having made this mistake, she ought to have the simple decency to remain indoors in her bathrobe, where she will not depress the entire community with the spectacle of her bulky contours.

2 *How to Keep Your Husband Believing That You Are Still the Same Enchanting Girl He Married* First you set aside a half hour in the late afternoon to put your hair up in pin curls and—no, this is ridiculous. I don't believe one word of it. Of course you're not the enchanting girl he married. How could you be—with those kids, and that dog racing through the house, and practically no help, and a washer that's always on the blink? And don't tell me about Mrs. Skylark; that woman probably *lives* at Elizabeth Arden's.

Besides, why should *you* be all that enchanting? How does *he* look these days? Is *he* still the lean and handsome athlete who first caught your girlish fancy? And was he even embarrassed when you had to bring back all those size forty shorts and get size forty-two? Do you catch him poring over articles instructing him how to look younger and sprucer so he can make your little heart palpitate? Boy, that'll be the day!

Frankly, I'm weary of the whole business. It's true: beauty *is* only skin deep. From now on I'm going to stop struggling. I'm just going to develop my character and let it shine through my fine eyes.